Living In The Age
of
White Reparations
By
D T Pollard
Essence Bestselling Author
Follow D T Pollard https://twitter.com/dtpollard

http://DTPollard.com

1

Anger boiled over after something went terribly wrong in the United States of America in June of 2018. Images of migrant children confined in metal pens flooded across television screens after being taken from their parents who crossed the southern border of the United States by order of President Donald J. Trump. Migrant children from teenagers to babies were caught up in the separation from parents dragnet due to a zero tolerance policy that prosecuted 100% of people crossing the border by charging them with a misdemeanor for illegal entry into the country. With a backdrop of the United States government running internment camps for migrant children separated from their families, on June 19, 2018, President Donald J. Trump made a statement that should make those with a sense of history blood run cold when he sent out a tweet stating:

"Democrats are the problem. They don't care about crime and want illegal immigrants, no matter how bad they may be, to pour into and infest our Country, like MS-13. They can't win on their terrible policies, so they view them as potential voters!"

The President of the United States referred to illegal immigrants as an infestation like insects, rodents or or other vermin. Humans live in or inhabit a country, but typically infestations are viewed as destructive and must be removed. The most powerful man on the planet characterized migrants coming to the United States in subhuman terms. In the all too instructive past, Adolf Hitler called Jews serpents and we know the rest of that tragic story. I pondered how we got to a place in the history of the United States that seemed unimaginable in the 21$^{st}$ century and then a prior conversation between two men came to mind?

"Nobody cares about a White man anymore," I overheard an older White man say who was talking to his male companion while eating pizza in a restaurant.

I thought, "What happened to cause some White men in America to feel they were victimized, ignored and oppressed? My ancestors were brought to the United States by force while shackled as human freight in the cargo hold of slave ships, possibly by the forebears of those two men. Then it dawned on me how this odd situation developed over hundreds of years of change since the inception of a new nation. The United States had the audacity to actually attempt to live up to its guiding principles over the years, although often at great cost in blood and treasure."

While those two men I encountered in a pizza shop were sharing their angst with each other about feeling marginalized in today's America, there were others harboring similar feelings of reduced stature while seething with anger and resentment. A subset of White men who believed in their inherent racial superiority over others felt they had been unjustly deposed from their rightful perch at the top of the economic, political and social hierarchy in the United States. While far less than a majority, many White men felt others had been artificially advantaged to their detriment. The faction of White men that harbored feelings of diminishment was vocal.

After eight years of a Black man serving as President of the United States, angry White men were a force desperate to burst forth from the darkness of birtherism and alt-Right internet hate groups. At its core, the United States had entered a period when individuals fought to regain or retain their personal definitions of dignity, but some felt their personal self worth rested on an outdated concept of superiority based upon race, gender or religion. Those with a viewpoint that African Americans, Hispanics, LBGTQ and even women had risen at their expense wanted payback because the United States tried to live up to its creed:

We hold these truths to be self-evident, that all men are created equal, that they are endowed by their Creator with certain unalienable Rights, that among these are Life, Liberty and the pursuit of Happiness.

(First sentence of second paragraph in the Declaration of Independence of the United States of America adopted on July 4th, 1776 by the United States Congress)

The founding fathers of the United States of America and framers of the Constitution adopted the Declaration of Independence on July 4th 1776. The men that set forth the framework that would still guide the United States centuries later were White and many were slave owners, including Thomas Jefferson who wrote the words, 'all men are created equal'. Almost two hundred and fifty years after the adoption of the Declaration of Independence, backlash from years of effort to bring those lofty words into complete reality would usher in a national leader who would rise to the highest office in the United States by answering the cries from those demanding White reparations for perceived wrongs committed against them. The eight years of the Presidency of Barak Obama, the first African American President, allowed a unique frustration to fester within some in the nation who thought too much change had occurred. A clarion call captured the devotion of those longing for things to be set right came from a man shouting he would make America great again and those feeling victimized knew exactly what that meant to them.

A portion of the population demanded restoration of the United States they once knew and loved from the past when they sat atop the socioeconomic structure in an unquestioned fashion. An angry undercurrent of sentiment existed, although far from universal, that White men were being denied their birthright superiority as descendants of those who founded the United States in favor of others the Constitutional framers never conceived as being created equal to them. In short, even though they didn't realize it, the loudest and angriest voices wanted nothing short of White reparations.

Most of the people demanding to take their country back would stridently deny they wanted reparations for transgressions committed against them because reparations were almost always thought of something descendants of slaves discussed. In general, reparations are to meant to compensate for wrongs done to a victimized person or group such as was often cited in the case of slavery. In the twenty first century we lived in an era where a segment of the populace that had benefitted the most from the efforts of historically oppressed populations felt disadvantaged. It must also be noted that most of the intense anger burning inside those longing for a return to a state of inequality harbored beliefs of their inherent racial superiority combined with a zero sum view of prosperity.

Given the history of the United States it seemed absurd for anyone from the class of individuals that was on top throughout the existence of the country to assert they had been victimized by social and cultural progress. To be clear, not all who supported Trump for President felt wronged by social change and the vast majority did not. Many Trump supporters voted their political party interests and others just wanted someone to fight for their desire for a better life in terms of jobs, earnings and opportunities in areas of the country left behind in a changing global economy. Trump spoke to what many saw as the forgotten men and women living in the decimated industrial heart of the United States that was littered with shuttered factories.

That vast group of people desiring better lives for themselves and their children took Trump's pledge to address their plights to heart and begrudgingly ignored much of his other culturally toxic rhetoric in hopes of him keeping his promise to bring their jobs back. For some people desperate to see a positive change in their economic situations, voting for Donald Trump was a Hail Mary pass. If Trump kept his word and brought some jobs back to beleaguered areas, then it would be a win, but if he didn't, he would not be any different than previous Presidents.

There was another group attracted to Trump because of his vitriolic pronouncements that no other politician would dare say in front of a national audience. Trump's promises to keep Muslims out of the country, build a southern border wall to keep illegal immigrants out of the Unites States and withdraw from international agreements sent a positive signal to a particular segment of the population. Trump's prior efforts in smearing the first Black President, Barack Obama, as an illegitimate President by charging he was not born in the United States was well known and gave him bonafides with those clinging to deep seated beliefs of White supremacy. Donald Trump was the messiah for racists lurking in the shadows, hiding behind keyboards spewing hate and embracing racial hatred in private because he gave them freedom to emerge from the darkness with their extreme views on full display. Like vampires shunning daylight suddenly free to walk with their fangs exposed at high noon, many felt liberated to show their fellow Americans how they really felt about true equality among men.

The hardcore group Trump unleashed harbored a certain view of the world that perceived any diminishment of their social or economic stature as being caused by elevation of others that should be below them based upon their gene pool. White supremacists and those with White supremacy viewpoints, although they would never admit it, wanted reparations extracted from Blacks, Hispanics, Muslims and any other groups that intruded upon their American dream. Trump exploited that desire for economic, social and racial retribution to his benefit. Trump's promise to make America great again was interpreted by racists as him imposing policies to right wrongs done to aggrieved White Americans due their decline because of the rise of Blacks, browns and undeserving others in the United States. In the opinion of those cherry picking their patriotism, The Declaration of Independence and Constitution worked too well as guiding principles because too many in the underclass were now counted as equally created men and that needed to be rectified. Blacks, Mexicans, Muslims, gays, transgenders, Asians, immigrants, other ethnic minorities and even women were in the crosshairs of blame as having slowly eroded the stature of White men espousing inherent superiority by virtue of their very existence.

2

The words "all men are created equal" is that well known phrase in the second paragraph of the Declaration of Independence of the United States of America adopted on July 4, 1776 and resulted in centuries of oppression, turmoil, and bloodshed over who would be considered equally created men. Many societal upheavals, equal rights movements and election outcomes would revolve around inclusion or exclusion into the club of equally created men. Being considered an equally created man meant the ability to freely pursue the bounty and opportunities the United States offered, but that would not come easily to many in the nation.

Slavery, Black Codes, lynching and Jim Crow laws were inflicted on African Americans who were brought to the United States by force to toil in uncompensated slave bondage. Native Americas were slaughtered and forced onto reservations after newcomers came to their land and claimed it as their own. Japanese Americans were placed into internment camps during World War II. Many Hispanics that came to the United States to seek better lives were often marginalized and relegated to off the record status that impacted their future prospects. Women did not originally have the right to vote. When the words stating that all men are created equal were written, it was considered to be an exclusive club comprised of White men only, but that would change much to the displeasure of many.

The Declaration of Independence guaranteed that over time, if the United Stated held true to its promise, the door would be open for every citizen to fully enjoy what the new nation had to offer, but many resisted and attempted to reserve prime opportunities for their kind only. Many were willing to kill and die to keep the club of equally created men, exclusively male and White. Sadly, in order to preserve the ultimate underclass through slavery, many felt it was worth destroying the United States altogether and went to war against the nation itself. History taught that continued oppression of others was a hard and dirty undertaking given that the oppressed tend to resist involuntary deprivation while watching their oppressors prosper at their expense. The natural instinct of any group was to rise up in order to create better lives for themselves and their offspring and if that meant engaging in prolonged struggle against those attempting to hold them back, so it was.

The structure of the United States of America was truly amazing and it was not clear that the founding fathers realized how extraordinary the governing framework they implemented was in the world. Ethic, gender and religious groups relegated to less than full equal status at the nation's inception used the very words adopted by our government to declare its independence to justify lifting restrictions based upon factors such as race, gender, religion and sexual orientation. The history of the United States is written in blood for African Americans, Native Americans and LBGTQ communities. Women were not allowed to vote for much of the nation's history and still lack wage parity with men. Hispanic Americans, especially those from Mexico and nations farther south (brown) endured a special kind of scorn from those seeking scapegoats for their social or economic struggles. It was no surprise that Donald Trump's characterization of Mexican immigrants as drug smugglers and rapists was a clarion call to extreme elements that he was their champion to right what was wrong in their worldview. Ku Klux Klan members, Neo Nazis and alt right supporters openly supported Trump's candidacy. Those with White Supremacy mindsets saw Donald Trump as their champion and threw in their lot with those drawn to him based upon their political party affiliation or economic concerns.

Trump won the election and became President of the United States although he lost the popular vote by millions. Some saw Trump's victory as their opportunity to revive their version of the Civil War that never ended in their minds along with a chance to extract a form of reparations to remind everyone who should be counted as equal in America.

After Trump's election we found ourselves living in an altered version of the United States that was reminiscent of a time past when law enforcement inflicted official racial harassment upon minorities on demand, women's rights were rolled back and open racial hatred came from the highest office in the land. Religious bigotry was on full display and misogynistic behavior was excused by national religious leaders in lieu of social agenda gains. An assault was taking place in broad daylight on the Declaration of Independence, Constitution of the United States and democracy itself by a President of the United States and a subset of his followers. Everyone watched while the Constitution was inserted into a shedder with the President's finger on the activate button. Trump continued to pave the way for increased social unrest in the areas of racial hate, bigotry and retribution by members of the public against those they saw as undesirable.

Sowing division was not usually the practice of a President elected to serve all citizens in the United States, but by his actions Trump decided to cater only to the most extreme elements of his support base that elected him into office. Trump went out of his way to demonstrate to his followers in rhetoric and law that he was with them by showing which groups he thought deserved his scorn.

Trump targeted Black professional athletes kneeling during the national anthem to protest law enforcement treatment of African Americans and twisted it into a display of lack of patriotism for the country. Trump stepped up immigrant deportation efforts and his Attorney General even emphasized separating children from their parents who were detained for illegally entering the country. Trump denigrated protected status immigrants from certain nations by saying they were from shithole countries.

The list of actions taken by President Trump that gave a green light for his diehard supporters to follow suit was long, but the message was received and individuals began taking actions against their fellow Americans they thought needed to be put in their place. White reparations were in progress and while not monetary, they satisfied a desire for some to soothe their egos by feeling things were being put in proper order with their guy in charge after going completely off the rails when Obama was in office. The psychological payback to some of those taking their racial wrath out on others they felt empowered to police was hugely satisfying to many engaged in their moments of vengeance. The superiority of the wounded White man would be clear once more because the President of the

United States was with them and said they were fine people.

Of course there were far more Americans of every stripe watching in horror as they felt the soul of the nation was at stake and one of our stopgaps for protection from a runaway President, The United States Congress, failed to push back because Republican members chose their political party loyalty over their Constitutional duty. The ability of the United States to survive with its moral center intact was being sorely tested by a panicked pushback from a core group to the reality that The United States of America was projected to be a majority minority country by 2044 according to the United States Census Bureau. Simply stated, in order for Trump to fulfill his promise to make America great again he would have to literally halt the progression of decades' long demographic changes and turn back time to an earlier social construct of America.

# Projecting Majority-Minority

**Non-Hispanic Whites May No Longer Comprise Over 50 Percent of the U.S. Population by 2044**

Percent Minority by Age Group: 2014 to 2060

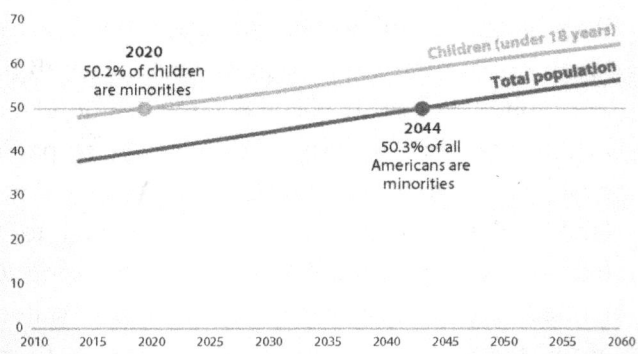

https://www.census.gov/content/dam/Census/newsroom/releases/2015/cb15-tps16_graphic.pdf

3

The United States had a long history of minority populations being relegated to positions that did not allow them to share fully in the bounty of this nation while contributing greatly to its growth. Often when an abhorrent chapter in American history was finally closed there was little done to compensate those harmed by those practices and that occurred in the case of slavery.

General Sherman issued Special Field Order #15 after the end of the Civil War that stated 400,000 acres along the South Carolina, Georgia and Florida coasts would be seized and set aside for freed slaves in 40 acre lots. Special Order #15 was implemented, but reversed by President Andrew Johnson. Thousands of formers slaves were evicted from land distributed to them in the early in 1865 during the latter portion of 1865. One case where reparations were paid was for Japanese Americans sent to internment camps during World War II. In February 1942, two months after the Japanese attacked Pearl Harbor, President Roosevelt issued Executive Order 9066 that ordered all persons in the United States outside of the Pacific military zone to be relocated inland. Japanese Americans and others of Japanese decent in the United States were forced to liquidate their assets before being sent to multiple internment camps in the nation's interior far away from their homes. Over forty years later in 1988 the H.R.442 - Civil Liberties Act of 1987 was signed into law by President Ronald Reagan and paid $20,000 to persons of Japanese descent sent to internment camps during World War II. According to information contained in the United States government archives approximately 117,000 persons of Japanese ancestry were targeted for internment at the time the relocation act was signed.

https://www.archives.gov/education/lessons/japanese-relocation
https://www.congress.gov/bill/100th-congress/house-bill/442

Native Americans were forced off their ancestral lands. President Andrew Jackson signed the Indian Removal Act on May 28, 1830. On December 6, 1830 President Jackson addressed Congress and said, "It gives me pleasure to announce to Congress that the benevolent policy of the Government, steadily pursued for nearly thirty years, in relation to the removal of the Indians beyond the white settlements is approaching to a happy consummation. Two important tribes have accepted the provision made for their removal at the last session of Congress, and it is believed that their example will induce the remaining tribes also to seek the same obvious advantages."

https://www.loc.gov/rr/program/bib/ourdocs/Indian.html

Women were not counted among equally created men and did not gain the right to vote on a national basis until 1920. Many White women issued the same cry for White reparations as White men during the 2016 election cycle, although the promise to make America great again was not for them either, but they could experience collateral benefits. Trump demonstrated by his personal behavior, history and statements that women were transactional objects of pleasure in his mind, but less than an equally created man. White women who engaged in reaping psychological reparations from minorities they abhorred needed to realize they were pawns used by Trump and his Republican supporters to garner support from far right religious leaders  through greater legislative control of their bodies in relation to the abortion issue.

The seemingly simple ideals embodied in those powerful words in the Declaration of Independence went far beyond the ability of the founding fathers to imagine how the new nation they created would transform over time. Some may disagree, but the Declaration of Independence was written with the social and political power structure of the time in mind.  In 1776 White men held all of the social, economic and political power. Living up to the high bar set forth in the Declaration of Independence would ensure that American society would continually change and set up a never ending struggle over who would be counted as equally created.

Black people in the newly formed United States were not considered to be among those equally created men referred to in the Declaration of Independence. Black people were slaves and classified as the property of their owners. Indigenous people who were here when the European colonists arrived were not considered to be citizens of the new nation at all and did not count among those with the right to pursue happiness. White women were not allowed to vote and apparently were not created equal, but derived their social and economic standing from their men. Even brilliant minds in 1776 could not conceive of a world two and a half centuries later. In the twenty first century a whole host of people with roots from all over the world were now solidly United States citizens and were never even imagined to be part of the group endowed with certain unalienable rights when those words were initially written, but almost two hundred and fifty years was a long passage of time and conditions changed.

Some descendants of individuals who found themselves in a strange land they claimed as their own chafed at the prospect that they were not automatically at the front of the line. The reality was lost on some of those protesting the loudest that their family lineage in the United States may have begun long after African slaves were brought to the country and they certainly have shallower family roots than Native Americans. Although White Americans of various ancestral backgrounds were now considered equally created, that was not the case when their ancestors first set foot on American soil in the past. Irish, Italian, Poles, Hungarian, Jews and some other European immigrants were not considered White when they arrived. In order for those new European immigrants to be accepted as White, which meant equal, they had to attain a certain level of social status and wealth as a group. Eventually the European newcomers were accepted as White although some latent hatred and stereotyping still existed even among ethnicities. Regardless of how the angry group attained their claim on what they felt was the right to be above those considered not worthy, it was clear to them that something went terribly wrong. The reality was that some of those making the most noise while expressing their displeasure with their current state had not witnessed the great America they longed for since the days of their parents or grandparents. By the time the current group of disgruntled individuals were ready for their turn to grasp the brass ring it was gone, had moved to another area or required a different skill set they did not possess. An unknown number of White men felt injustices like affirmative action had occurred over time that resulted in feelings of economic oppression, diminished social stature and resentment at the elevation of others over them and it was time for that not only to end, but to be reversed.

The word reparations never crossed the lips of those seething with anger about feelings that others usurped their American dream, but suddenly they felt free to express those sentiments openly for the first time in decades. A new age of incivility would be unleashed with the leader of the free world's blessing.

3

Throughout history nations rose and fell, often by failing to reign in leaders that led them down destructive paths. The United States of America was poised to follow in the footsteps of The Roman Empire, The Soviet Union and, dare say it, Nazi Germany if President Donald J. Trump was not removed from office, rebuked by Republican leaders in Congress or politically handcuffed by Democrats taking control of Congress in 2018. Donald J. Trump was poisoning the heart of America. In Donald Trump's vision of America your value was determined by what you were, not who you were. In Donald Trump's America unless you were a wealthy White man or part of his rabid and cheering 33% to 40+% support base that he said would not leave him even if he shot someone in the street, you had a specific role in Trump's mind. There was no need to speculate about how Trump felt about you if you were someone other than a White man because he told the world with words out of his mouth and his tweets. Trump let women, immigrants of color, Puerto Ricans, Native Americans, African Americans, Muslims, Mexicans, etc. know exactly where they fit in his world.

Sitting as the elected leader of a nation comprised of immigrants and their offspring, on January 11, 2018 during a meeting dealing with immigration issues, Trump reportedly said the following when the subject of restoring temporary protected status to immigrants from certain countries in particular El Salvador, Haiti and African countries:

"Why are we having all these people from shithole countries come here?" Trump reportedly said. It was also reported by those in the room that Trump said we needed more immigrants from places like Norway. Trump was alleged to have singled out that Haiti be left out of any new arrangement and that Haitians already in the United States under the program should be taken out of the country. The countries listed below were on the protected status list at the time of the meeting between Trump and sitting U.S. Senators.

- El Salvador
- Haiti
- Honduras
- Nepal
- Nicaragua
- Somalia
- Sudan
- South Sudan
- Syria
- Yemen

Source: U.S. Citizenship and Immigration Services - https://www.uscis.gov/humanitarian/temporary-protected-status

A current United States Senator, who was in the meeting, confirmed that Donald Trump, the sitting President of the United States, made his "shithole countries" remark from the Oval Office in the White House.

Donald Trump was pulling the office of the President of the United States down to new lows on almost a daily basis when it seemed he could go no lower from a previous outrageous statement or tweet. The President of the United States had traditionally set a high moral tone for the country and stood for a certain type of ethical leadership the rest of the world looked to as a guidepost, but Trump was tearing that down and it might never be completely restored.

Donald Trump, as President, called primarily Black professional football players protesting to draw attention to African Americans killed at the hands of law enforcement, sons-of-bitches. Trump, as President, used a White House ceremony honoring Native American military veterans, Navajo code talkers, to strike out at a political opponent by using the name of Pocahontas as a slur.

There is a caution for White women cheering as part of Trump's 33% core supporters, wake up! Donald Trump told you with words out of his own mouth how he felt about you. In Trump's mind and apparently in reality, women were there to serve his carnal needs if they were attractive enough, of course. Trump said if he saw an attractive woman he would just start kissing them without permission. Trump said women would allow him to do anything and he wanted because he was famous, "grab them by the pussy", those were Trump's words describing what he actually did, so sober up and think of your daughters' futures.

On Friday September 22, 2017 the United States of America experienced another low point in its history in Huntsville, Alabama as the 45th President of the United States, Donald Trump, stood behind a podium with the Presidential seal customarily affixed and called African American men sons-of-bitches. To be clear, Trump did not specifically say the people he used the derogatory term to describe were black, but he targeted professional football players kneeling during the national anthem to protest police treatment of Blacks in the United States and that group was composed of predominately African American men. Since Trump didn't say Black men, his supporters could claim his vulgar remark was about disrespect for our flag and country which was a cynical and tired way of denying the blatant racism of his slur. Trump, the 45th President of the United States, could have been the 45th Governor of Alabama, George Wallace, uttering similar words that night in Huntsville, Alabama. As a lifelong Black man with six decades invested as an American from birth, I've heard hundreds of years of accumulated labels attached to people of color from Whites with superior attitudes designed to keep them on top of the socioeconomic mountain in the United States.

Donald Trump painted a word picture in front of a receptive White audience in Alabama when he said, "Wouldn't you love to see one of these NFL owners, when somebody disrespects our flag, to say, 'Get that son-of-a-bitch off the field right now. Out! He's fired. He's fired!' The crowd roared. Trump knew exactly what he was doing, but while he was stirring up resentment fueled racial hate excused by a cynical outrage over reflexive patriotism over the flag and national anthem, category 4 Hurricane Maria struck 3.5 million United States citizens two days earlier in Puerto Rico completely destroying the infrastructure of the island leaving them in desperation, but Trump was busy stirring the racial hatred pot in Alabama instead of focusing on planning for delivering maximum relief efforts.

What Trump did in Alabama and his lack of focus on ensuring effective relief efforts in Puerto Rico were connected in a sad manner. Trump would later call the 3.5 million American citizens in Puerto Rico lazy while they were suffering from the effects of a devastating hurricane by stating they wanted everything done for them. Of course, Trump called Puerto Ricans slothful for asking the same treatment from the federal government as Texas and Florida received when they were struck by earlier hurricanes in 2017. Let us not forget that Trump kicked off his Presidential campaign by labeling many Hispanic immigrants from Mexico as murders and rapists. Trump's previous public statements about Hispanics forecasted his attitude toward the desperate situation of Puerto Ricans, who were American citizens, in a different light. Trump simply did not consider Puerto Ricans equal to citizens of Florida and Texas that suffered similar disastrous situations. Trump even had the nerve to downplay the scope of the disaster in Puerto Rico by comparing it to Hurricane Katrina. Trump said Katrina was a real disaster because thousands of lives were lost compared to a double digit total reported at the time in Puerto Rico. Months later in 2018 it was reported that thousands may have died as a result of Hurricane Maria

Trump made his statement about multimillionaire Black athletes protesting police treatment of Blacks to a group in an area of the nation that may have harbored resentment of those they felt were ungrateful for what they had and still had the nerve to complain about treatment of fellow Blacks in this country, but I heard something else. I heard a rich White man, who happened to be President, telling other rich White men, who owned the teams, to get their niggers in line or I will hurt you in your pocketbook by turning your White fans against you. I heard with my seasoned racial dog whistle translation filter the terms uppity niggers, cocky nigger and boy. I heard a rich White man use the lofty platform of the Presidency of the United States and take it to a very low place by telling wealthy Black athletes that their communities looked up to that even though you have attained your American dream, you're still just a nigger. I heard a rich White man hide behind the bully pulpit of the United States Presidency and call the mothers of proud young Black men bitches. I also witnessed the President of the United States take the issue of violence against Blacks by police and trample upon it with the "standing for the national anthem out of respect" fake issue he injected into the national conversation, in other words, owners get your rich niggers in line and tell them to shut up and entertain us. The national media fell right in line and even conducted polls to determine how Americans felt about players standing for the national anthem instead of focusing on why Black players were kneeling in the first place.

Let us coin a new term, non-White in the USA. The President of the United States called Blacks sons of bitches. The President of the United States called Mexicans murderers and rapists. The President of the United States said Puerto Ricans didn't want to help themselves as they struggled to survive after a category 4 hurricane devastated their island. The President of the United States said migrants were infesting the country. While President Donald Trump said those things about people of color, he said neo Nazis, the Ku Klux Klan and other White Supremacists had fine people among them after they gathered in Charlottesville, North Carolina causing unbelievable chaos and death.

What is it like to be non-White in Trump's United States of America? Even if you didn't ask I'll tell you anyway, even if you don't care or want to know. I'm Black, like the men President Trump called sons of bitches and I assure you that I don't consider myself to be the son of a bitch, so back at you Trump.

Being non-White in the United States of American meant you had to develop a compartmentalized way of thinking in order to maintain your sanity. Being non-White in the USA meant you might have sent your child to a public school named after men who fought against the United States during the Civil War, like Jefferson

Davis or Robert E. Lee in order to maintain slavery of African Americans. Being non-White in the USA meant you witnessed exceptional non-White performers in sports and entertainment bypassed for commercial success outside of their vocations because they are deemed unmarketable to preferred demographics. Being non-White in the USA meant physical features such as the plump lips or prominent buttocks of Black women were grotesque or ghetto until adopted by Whites and then they became fashionable. Being non-White in the USA meant you celebrated the election of the first non-White President and then watched him being treated like a runaway slave with birthers asking him to prove he was born in the United States and Constitutionally eligible to hold the office. Being non-White in the USA meant drug epidemics like crack were crime problem in non-White areas, but became a public health issue when the Opiod epidemic hit White America. Being non-White in the USA meant you witnessed the election of the 45th President of the United States, Donald Trump, who championed the birther movement against the 44th President, Obama, which smeared the first Black President of the United States. Being non-White in the USA meant you watched a former Grand Wizard of the Ku Klux Klan, David Duke, say, 'We are determined to take our country back. We are going to fulfill the promises of Donald Trump. That's what we believed in, that's why we voted for Donald Trump', during a White Nationalist event that resulted in the death of a woman. Being non-White in the USA meant you had a President that White Supremacists considered to be their champion in the White House.

Being non-White in the USA has always carried the caveat that you may put more into being a patriotic American than you got out of it. Throughout much of the history of the United States Blacks toiled in industry, competed in sports and died fighting wars to make this country what it is today, but often were not able to fully enjoy its bounty. Some elements in this society will have a reflexive recoil reaction and say if you don't like it here, then leave. As a Black person you may also hear the reply of why don't you just go back to Africa. That last reply is particularly insane because most African Americans had never been to Africa and were born in the United States. I had some long lost ancestors that were taken from Africa against their will and brought to the United States shackled in the bottom of slave ships like animals and hence, I am here, but let us focus on the particular point of putting in more than you got of being an American as a Black person.

Slaves gave everything into building this nation against their will and without compensation. Untold numbers of a people ripped from their homeland, families and everything familiar in their lives were used, abused and killed to build the wealth of their captors. Freedom came for descendants of those former slaves as did the right to be counted as full citizens of the United States. The right of slave descendants to vote for those leading us politically in local and national government was won with blood just as was the legal right to sit in the same area as a White man to eat a meal at a restaurant. With all the history pain, blood and Black bodies swinging from trees, here we were over 150 years after slaves were freed in the United States when we all witnessed the 45th President of the United States choose not to condemn neo-Nazis, Ku Klux Klansmen and White Supremacists involved in a violent clash that resulted in many injuries and a death due to the use of a vehicle as a weapon.

So what happened to cause the United States to elect as President a man that reveled in stoking racial tension and division?   At the time of the drafting of the Declaration of Independence, which was a list of reasons why the newly formed United States had broken away from British rule, Black people, like me, were slaves and classified as property instead of equal to the adopters of the independence statement document. Over many years of progress and pain that included rape, murder, beatings and other nameless atrocities Blacks gained freedom and legal equality. A Black man, Barack Obama, was even elected as a two term President of the United States and served from 2009 until January 20, 2017 when he was succeeded by the 45th President of the United States, Donald J. Trump.

Just over six months after a Black man was succeeded as President of the United States, I watched images on my television screen of a gathering of White Supremacists gathered in Emancipation Park in Charlottesville, Virginia on August 12, 2017 clashing with those opposing their views in broad daylight. The fact the there was a clash between White Supremacists and a group opposing them was not the most surprising aspect of the incident. The most surprising and frightening fact about the group of White Supremacists that was composed of Neo-Nazis, KKK and others was their lack of any camouflage to hide their identity. Somehow it had become socially safe to be publically identifiable as a neo-Nazi or Ku Klux Klan member attacking counter protesters in the light of day. Nazis were one of the most notorious groups in history and under Adolf Hitler they executed 6 million Jews. Nazis felt other races were genetically inferior and neo-Nazis adopted their beliefs.

The Klan and neo-Nazis were not fans of anyone different from them. Events spiraled out of control in Charlottesville, Virginia to a point where a 20-year old White man plowed his car into a group of counter protesters resulting in numerous injuries and the death of a 32-year old woman. The man that committed that act of domestic terrorism was affiliated with the White nationalist protestors. When events occur like what happened in Charlottesville, Virginia, we as a nation look for guidance from the President of the United States to set a moral tone. President Donald Trump failed. Trump did not call out an act of domestic terrorism. Trump did not condemn the White Nationalists for their racism and violence and spread the blame equally on "many sides". Two days later after widespread condemnation of his weak original statement about the events in Charlottesville, Trump gave a revised statement that called out the Klan, neo-Nazis and White Supremacists by name for their racial hate, but he threw out a thin life line by saying other hate groups were undesirable also. Donald Trump was President of the United States and one day after delivering a forced and tersely delivered statement condemning White Supremacists, he expressed his true sentiments during an event to discuss infrastructure policy on August 15, 2017.

Barack Obama delivered a speech about race before he became President to calm fears among Whites after a sermon of his church pastor, Dr. Jeremiah Wright, were shown almost endlessly due to the racially charged language included that Obama's political opponents attempted to attached to him. Obama managed to calm the anxiety that existed and was elected President of the United States. Trump campaign speeches were designed to ratchet up racial tensions, but he delivered his signature diatribe in response to the White supremacist clash with counter protesters in Charlottesville, Virginia. Trump's rambling tirade in response to what happened in Charlottesville over efforts to remove Confederate Civil War monuments from a park cemented his place as the steadfast champion that stood up for the sliver of the population that still saw nobility in the cause the South fought against the United States to preserve.

4

Being non-White in the USA took on a new meaning on August 15, 2017 with an old stench as President Donald J Trump delivered remarks in what may be the most unique, troubling and frightening dialogue by a modern POTUS in this nation's history as he elevated racial hate groups to a status of legitimacy in American society.

Questions from reporters at the end of Donald Trump's remarks on infrastructure turned to the White Supremacist event in Charlottesville, Virginia on Saturday, August 13, 2017 that turned violent and the 45th President of the United States shocked the world with his unscripted remarks:

**Reporter's question**: Why do you think these CEOs are leaving your manufacturing council?

**President Trump**: Because they are not taking their job seriously as it pertains to this country. We want jobs, manufacturing in this country. If you look at some of those people that you're talking about, they're outside of the country. They're having a lot of their product made outside. If you look at Merck as an example. Take a look where, excuse me, excuse me. Take a look at where their product is made. It's made outside of our country. We want products made in the country. Now, I have to tell you, some of the folks that will leave, they are leaving out of embarrassment because they make their products outside and I've been lecturing them, including the gentleman that you're referring to, about you have to bring it back to this country. You can't do it necessarily in Ireland and all of these other places. You have to bring this work back to this country. That's what I want. I want manufacturing to be back into the United States so that American workers can benefit.

**Reporter's question**: Why did you wait so long to put that last statement out?

**President Trump**: I didn't wait long. I didn't wait long. I didn't wait long.

**Reporter's question**: It was at least 48 hours.

**President Trump**: I wanted to make sure, unlike most politicians, that what I said was correct. Not make a quick statement. The statement I made on Saturday, the first statement, was a fine statement. But you don't make statements that direct unless you know the fact. It takes a little while to get the facts. You still don't know the facts, and it's a very, very, ah, important process to me, and it's a very important statement, so I don't want to go quickly and just make a statement for the sake of making a political statement. I want to know the facts. If you go back to my... I brought it. I brought it. I brought it. As I said, remember this, Saturday, we condemn in the strongest possible terms this egregious display of hatred, bigotry and violence. It has no place in America, and then I went on from there. Now, here's the thing. Excuse me, excuse me. Take it nice and easy. Here's the thing. When I make a statement, I like to be correct. I want the facts. This event just happened. In fact, a lot of the event didn't even happen yet, as we were speaking.

This event just happened. Before I make a statement I need the facts, so I don't want to rush into a statement.

So, making the statement when I made it was excellent. In fact, the young woman, who I hear is a fantastic young woman, and it was on NBC, her mother wrote me and said, through I guess, Twitter, social media, the nicest things, and I very much appreciated that. I hear she was a fine, really actually an incredible young woman. But her mother on Twitter thanked me for what I said. And honestly, if the press were not fake and if it was honest, the press would have said what I said was very nice. But unlike you and unlike... excuse me, unlike you and unlike the media, before I make a statement I like to know the facts.

**President Trump**: They don't. They don't. They don't.

(Multiple reporters talk over each other.)

**President Trump**: Listen, how about, how about a couple of infrastructure questions?

**Reporter**: Was that terrorism, that event? Was that terrorism?

**President Trump**: Say it. What?

**Reporter**: The CEO of Wal-Mart said you missed a critical opportunity to help bring the country together. Did you?

**President Trump**: Not at all. I think the country... look, you take a look. I've created over a million jobs since I'm president. The country is booming, the stock market is setting records. We have the highest employment numbers we've ever had in the history of our country. We're doing record business. We have the highest levels of enthusiasm. So, the head of Wal-Mart, whom I know, who is a very nice guy, was making a political statement. I mean, I do it the same way. You know why? Because I want to make sure, when I make a statement that the statement is correct, and there was no way, there was no way of making a correct statement that early. I had to see the facts, unlike a lot of reporters, unlike a lot of reporters. (Reporter shouts a question about former Ku Klux Klan leader David Duke) I didn't know David Duke was there. I wanted to see the facts, and the facts as they started coming out were very well stated. In fact, everybody said his statement was beautiful. If he would have made it sooner, that would have been good. I couldn't have made it sooner because I didn't know all of the facts. Frankly, people still don't know all of the facts. It was very important... excuse me, excuse me. It was very important to me to get the facts out and correctly, because if I would have made a fast statement... and the first statement was made without knowing much other than what we were seeing. The second statement was made with knowledge, with great knowledge. There's still thing... excuse me, there's still things that people don't know. I want to make a statement with knowledge. I wanted to know the facts. Okay.

**Reporter**: Two questions. Was this terrorism and can you tell us how you're feeling about your chief strategist, Steve Bannon.

**President Trump**: Well, I think the driver of the car is a disgrace to himself, his family and this country, and that is, you can call it terrorism.

You can call it murder. You can call it whatever you want. I would just call it as the fastest one to come up with a good verdict. That's what I'd call it, because there is a question. Is it murder? Is it terrorism, and then you get into legal semantics. The driver of the car is a murderer and what he did was a horrible, horrible inexcusable thing.

**Reporter**: Can you tell us how you're feeling about your chief strategist, Mr. Bannon? Can you talk about that?

**President Trump**: Go ahead.

**Reporter**: I would echo Maggie's question. Steve Bannon has…

**President Trump**: I never spoke to Mr. Bannon about it.

**Reporter**: Can you tell us broadly… do you still have confidence in Steve?

**President Trump**: Well, we'll see. Look, look, I like Mr. Bannon, he's a friend of mine, but Mr. Bannon came on very late… you know that. I went through 17 senators, governors and I won all the primaries. Mr. Bannon came on very much later than that, and I like him, he's a good man. Ah, he is not a racist, I can tell you that. He's a good person, he actually gets a very unfair press in that regard. But we'll see what happens with Mr. Bannon, but he's a good person and I think the press treats him frankly very unfairly.

**Reporter**: Do you have confidence in him?

**A different reporter**: John McCain has called on you to defend your national security adviser H.R. McMaster against (unintelligible) attacks.

**President Trump**: I have already done it. I did it the last time.

**Reporter**: And he called on you again to…

**President Trump**: Senator McCain? Senator McCain? You mean the one who voted against Obamacare?

**Reporter**: And he said-

**President Trump**: Who is Senator- You mean Senator McCain who voted against us getting good health care?

**Reporter**: Senator McCain said that the alt-right is behind these attacks, and he linked that same group to those who perpetrated the attack in Charlottesville.

**President Trump**: Well, I don't know. I can't tell you. I'm sure Senator McCain must know what he's talking about. But when you say the alt-right...uh, define alt-right to me. You define it. Go ahead.

**President Trump**: No, define it for me. Come on, let's go.

**Reporter**: Senator McCain defined them as the same groups.

**President Trump**: OK. What about the alt-left that came charging at-

**President Trump**: Excuse me, what about the alt-left that came charging at the, as you say, the alt-right. Do they have any semblance of guilt?

**President Trump**: Let me ask you this. What about the fact they came charging — that they came charging, with clubs in their hands, swinging clubs? Do they have any problem? I think they do.

So, you know, as far as I'm concerned, that was a horrible, horrible day-

**President Trump**: Wait a minute. I'm not finished. I'm not finished, fake news. That was a horrible day.

**Reporter**: Is it the same level as neo-Nazis?

**President Trump**: I will tell you something. I watched those very closely, much more closely than you people watched it, and you have, ah. You had a group on one side that was bad and you had a group on the other side that was also very violent, and nobody wants to say that, but I'll say it right now. You had a group, you had a group on the other side that came charging in without a permit and they were very, very violent.

**President Trump**: Go ahead.

**Reporter**: Do you think what you call the alt-left is the same as neo-Nazis?

**President Trump**: Those people, all of those people, excuse me. I've condemned neo-Nazis. I've condemned many different groups, but not all of those people were neo-Nazis, believe me. Not all of those people were white supremacists, by any stretch.

**Reporter**: Well, white nationalists…

**President Trump**: Those people were also there because they wanted to protest the taking down of a statue of Robert E. Lee. So … Excuse me. And you take a look at some of the groups and you see and you'd know it if you were honest reporters, which in many cases you're not, but many of those people were there to protest the taking down of the statue of Robert E. Lee. So, this week it's Robert E. Lee. I noticed that Stonewall Jackson is coming down. I wonder is it George Washington next week and is it Thomas Jefferson the week after? You know, you really do have to ask yourself where does it stop, but they were there to protest- excuse me. you take a look the night before, they were there to protest the taking down of the statue of the Robert E. Lee. Infrastructure question? Go ahead.

**Reporter**: Should statues of Robert E. Lee stay up?

**President Trump**: I would say that's up to a local town, community, or the federal government depending on where it is located.

**Reporter**: Are you against the Confederacy?

**A different reporter**: How concerned are you about race relations in America and do you think things have gotten worse or better since you took office?

**President Trump**: I think they have gotten better, or the same, I, look. They've been frayed for a long time, and you can ask President Obama about that because he'd make speeches about it, but, I believe that the fact that I brought in, it will be soon, millions of jobs... you see where companies are moving back into our country... I think that's going to have a tremendous positive impact on race relations. We have companies coming back into our country, we have two car companies that just announced, we have FoxConn in Wisconsin just announced. We have many companies, I say pouring back into the country. I think that's going to

42

have a huge, positive impact on race relations. You know why? It's jobs. What people want now, they want jobs. They want great jobs with good pay and, when they have that, you watch how race relations will be, and I'll tell you, we're spending a lot of money on the inner cities. We're fixing the inner cities. We're doing far more than anybody's done with respect to the inner cities. It's a priority for me, and it's very important.

**Reporter**: Mr. President, are you putting what you're calling the alt-left and white supremacists on the same moral plane?

**President Trump**: I'm not putting anybody on a moral plane. What I'm saying is this: You had a group on one side and you had a group on the other and they came at each other with clubs and it was vicious and it was horrible and it was a horrible thing to watch, but there is another side. There was a group on this side …you can call them the left, you've just called them the left…that came violently attacking the other group, so you can say what you want but that's the way it is.

**Reporter**: Mr. President, your words…

**A different reporter**: You said there was hatred, there was violence on both sides. Are there…

**President Trump**: Well, I do think there's blame… Yes. I do think there's blame on both sides. You look at both sides. I think there's blame on both sides and I have no doubt about it and you don't have any doubt about it either and- and- and- and if you reported it accurately, you would say it.

**Reporter**: Heather Heyer died.(other reporters talking over each other)

**Reporter**: Neo-Nazis started this in Charlottesville. They showed up at Charlottesville, they...

**President Trump**: Excuse me.

**Reporter**: To protest the removal of that...

**President Trump**: You have some very bad people in that group, but you also had people that were very fine people on both sides. You had people in that group... Excuse me. Excuse me. I saw the same pictures as you did. You had people in that group that were there to protest the taking down of, to them, a very, very important statue and the renaming of a park from Robert E. Lee to another name.

**Reporter**: Do you support white nationalists, then?

**President Trump**: Well, George Washington was a slave owner. Was George Washington a slave owner? So, will George Washington now lose his status? Are we going to take down- Excuse me. Are we going to take down, are we going to take down statues to George Washington? How about Thomas Jefferson? What do you think of Thomas Jefferson? You like him?

**Reporter**: I do love Thomas Jefferson.

**President Trump**: OK, good. Well, are we going to take down the statue, because he was a major slave owner? Now, are we going to take down his statue? So, you know what? It's fine. You're changing history. You're changing culture and you had people, and I'm not talking about the neo-Nazis and the white nationalists because they should be condemned, totally. But you had many people in that group other than neo-Nazis and white nationalists, Okay? And the press has treated them absolutely unfairly. Now, in the other group also, you had some fine people, but you also had troublemakers and you see them come with the black outfits and with the helmets and with the baseball bats. You got a lot of bad people in the other group, too.

**Reporter**: Who was treated unfairly? Sir, I'm sorry I don't understand what you were saying. You were saying the press has treated white nationalists unfairly? I just don't understand what you were saying.

**President Trump**: No. No. There were people in that rally, and I looked the night before. If you look, there were people protesting very quietly the taking down of the statue of Robert E. Lee. I'm sure in that group there were some bad ones. The following day it looked like they had some rough, bad people: neo-Nazis, white nationalists, whatever you want to call them, but you had a lot of people in that group that were there to innocently protest, and very legally protest, because you know... I don't know if you know, they had a permit. The other group didn't have a permit. So, I only tell you this. There are two sides to a story. I thought what took place was a horrible moment for our country, a horrible moment, but there are two sides to the country. Does anybody have a final- does anybody- you have an infrastructure question.

**Reporter**: What makes you think you can get an infrastructure bill? You didn't get health care. You're-

**President Trump**: Well, you know, I'll tell you. We came very close with health care, unfortunately, John McCain decided to vote against it at the last minute. You'll have to ask John McCain why he did that. But we came very close to health care. We will end up getting health care, but we'll get the infrastructure and actually, infrastructure is something that I think we'll have bipartisan support on. I actually think, I actually think Democrats will go along with the infrastructure.

**Reporter**: Mr. President, have you spoken to the family, have you spoken to the family of the victim of the car attack?

**President Trump**: No, I'll be reaching out. I'll be reaching out.

**Reporter**: When will you be reaching out?

**President Trump**: I was very... I thought that the statement put out, the mother's statement; I thought was a beautiful statement. I must tell you, I was- it was something that I really appreciated. I thought it was terrific, and really under the- under the kind of stress that she's under and the heartache that she's under, I thought putting out that statement to me was really something I won't forget. Thank you all very much. Thank you. Thank you.

**First reporter**: What about the Nazis who support you?

**Second Reporter**: Do you plan on going to Charlottesville, Mr. President?

**Third Reporter**: Do you think you're helping to heal the nation?

**President Trump**: I own a house in Charlottesville. Does anyone know I own a house in Charlottesville?

**Reporter**: Where is it?

**President Trump**: Oh, boy, it's going to be- it's in Charlottesville, you'll see.

**Reporter**: Is it in the winery or something?

**President Trump**: It's a- it is the winery.

**President Trump**: I mean, I know a lot about Charlottesville. Charlottesville is a great place that's been very badly hurt over the last couple of days. I own- I own actually one of the largest wineries in the United States that's in Charlottesville.

**Reporter**: What do you think needs to be done to overcome the racial divides in this country?

**President Trump**: Well I really think jobs can have a big impact. I think if we continue to create jobs, over a million, substantially more than a million... and you can see just the other day, the car companies coming in with fox- you know, FoxConn. I think if we continue to create jobs at levels that I'm- that I'm creating jobs, I think that's going to have a tremendous impact, positive impact on race relations.

**Reporter**: And what you said today, how do you think that will impact the racial, sort of conflict today?

**President Trump**: Because people are going to be working, they're going to be making a lot of money, much more money than they ever thought possible.

**President Trump**: And the other thing, very important, I believe wages will start going up. They haven't gone up for a long time. I believe wages now, because the economy is doing so well with respect to employment and unemployment, I believe wages will start to go up. I think that will have a tremendously positive impact on race relations. Thank you.

5

The psychological whiplash of transitioning from Barack Obama as President to Donald Trump was both mind boggling and disheartening. To hear the President of the United States declare that a White supremacist march featuring individuals carrying flaming torches while chanting "Jews will not replace us" and the Nazi chant "blood and soil" was simply a peaceful protest with fine people involved. Blood and Soil was a Nazi ideology that focused on White racial purity and was instrumental in painting German Jews as less than ideal Germans. Blut und Boden is Blood and Soil in German and makes sense when you realize it was tied to German farmers being elevated as national heroes due to their German-Nordic (White) bloodline and the land they were connected to. The Blood and Soil ideology was use to smear Jewish Germans and justified expanding into lands outside of German control because of historical Blood and Soil affiliations. The Holocaust in which six million Jews were killed by the Nazis during World War II was one of the legacies of Blood and Soil, but Trump said both sides were at fault in Charlottesville, North Carolina where a young woman was killed by a White Supremacist ramming his car into a crowd of counter protestors.

The thing about the Charlottesville event was the multi-headed hydra of racial hate it represented. President Donald Trump's failure to unequivocally condemn the actions of the hate groups involved in the Charlottesville, Virginia confrontation and then spread blame clearly emboldened those with White supremacy attitudes. Charlottesville was a seminal event in the history of the United States from a modern cultural and political standpoint. Charlottesville should stand alongside some of the other racially based social eruptions that have occurred throughout the history of the nation.

One of the differences in Charlottesville was that it was not a backlash against some act of law enforcement against an African American citizen as was in recent years. The outbreak of hate and violence in Charlottesville did not take place against the backdrop of a struggling minority neighborhood or run down business district. Charlottesville did not feature the stark contrast of a predominately Black group of protestors versus uniformed law enforcement. The clash in Charlottesville was a clash of backward looking racist White supremacy ideology against the forward facing ideology of inclusiveness and progress. The world was flipped around as a group of White antagonists spewing racial hate against Blacks, Jews and the idea of inclusiveness encountered pushback from a multiracial group opposing them espousing the America described in the Declaration of Independence.

The lone direct death in the Charlottesville protest was a young White woman protesting against the White supremacists when one of the alt-Right members used his automobile as a weapon and drove it into a group of the counter protestors. Two law enforcement officers also lost their lives when the helicopter they used to patrol the event crashed. Everything about what took place in Charlottesville served as a crucible for the period the United States was entering after the election of Donald Trump as President of the United States. Up until the outbreak of violence in Charlottesville, Trump had ignored the larger group of American citizens that voted for his opponent than for him. Trump lost the popular vote by approximately three million votes. In the past when a President came into office with a weak mandate based upon the election results he would reach out to those who voted for his opponent and attempt to unite the country. Donald Trump not only did little to broaden his base, he actually drilled downward past his soft supporters who voted for him for party or economic reasons to solidify support among those attracted to his retrograde racial message. Everyone held their breaths in anticipation of Trump's response to Charlottesville.

Trump could have breached much of the gulf between himself and those that opposed him if he had strongly repudiated in no uncertain terms the actions, White supremacy ideology and hate groups that caused the chaos in Charlottesville, but he shocked the nation. American citizens watched in disbelief as the President of the United States in the 21$^{st}$ century struggled in real time and failed to fully condemn racial hate. Trump bolstered the positions of those hanging onto some rose colored view of the Confederate cause in the Civil War by lamenting efforts to remove Confederate statues from public spaces. Donald Trump even attempted to draw a moral equivalence between some of the slave owning founding fathers and Confederate notables who fought against the United States to maintain slavery eighty five years after the inception of the nation. Some began to openly ponder what it really meant for the United States to have a President that displayed open animosity for the founding principle of all men being created equal. It was one thing to have political policy differences with a President, but it was totally unique for a large segment of the population to have a difference in how they viewed race as a factor in how individual Americans were viewed compared to the POTUS.

Many citizens who were prepared to give Trump a chance to prove them wrong on the views he held on race, that appeared to be validated by media accounts, were convinced after his response to a White supremacist fueled melee in Virginia. It was one thing to be an individual totally opposed to the type of racist attitude coming from the President of the United States who was not a member of a minority group, but to a non-White American it was multiple times more offensive. Non-White Americans had to reconcile with the reality that the President of the United States apparently did not consider them to be equal to him.

Trump defenders would argue that there had not been a direct statement that could be pointed to when he directly said non-Whites where not equal to White Americans. Clever racists never directly state non-Whites were inferior, but their followers would. The perfect example was when Trump called predominately Black millionaire professional football players a vulgarity for protesting against police brutality against African Americans by kneeling during the playing of the national anthem. Trump said what he did, but the implication was a statement on wealth and power. The following was one view of what Trump meant:

"Team owners you better get your uppity niggers in line or I will wreck your profits. I don't care that they were protesting police brutality against African Americans because my followers believe what I tell them. If I say they were disrespecting the flag and America, that's what my base will believe. My core supporters are struggling and already don't like the idea that those niggers are making millions of dollars, but they still work for you. I'm showing them that no matter how much they make, they still don't own anything and can still be fired. You all decide how you are going to handle this, but don't fight me on this one because you will lose."

Some may say that the above interpretation was harsh, but it could have been worse, because the person that heard those words pulled from their own experience base. As a Black man that grew up and lived in the southern United States for six decades, my racist dog whistle decoder was fairly finely tuned. The team owners apparently got the message because before the next professional football season started they instituted a rule requiring players to stand at attention during the national anthem or stay in the locker room until the anthem was over if they wanted to protest. Some may ask what is wrong with standing for the national anthem and flag, but one of the things the flag stood for was freedom of speech and expression. Apparently the White supremacists in Charlottesville could shout Jews will not replace us and try to protect statues of individuals that committed the Constitutional definition of treason against the United States, but football players should not be allowed to kneel to protest police brutality against African Americans. Standing for the national anthem and flag should be a choice, not forced in the United States.

White supremacists took great comfort in having a President who boldly expressed from the highest office in the land views they previously kept in private or let fly while hiding behind an alias online. Seeing Trump attack a gold star Muslim family who lost their son while he was fighting for the United States gave solace to Muslim haters. Trump's ranting about building a southern border wall and characterizations of Mexicans as rapists, drug smugglers and animals pleased those blaming immigrants for their economic decline. Trump reserved his animal comments for the MS 13 gang whose members were primarily of Central American descent. While Trump could say he was specifically calling MS 13 member animals, it was really using the time worn practice of denigrating a wider group by targeting a negatively perceived subgroup out for criticism. The use of a proxy that was a member of a group, like immigrants, had been routinely used to cast wider aspersions upon an entire population, but still maintain plausible deniability. Trump seemed to be very adept in the art of race baiting and did it in a nuanced manner that caused speculation about if he had assistance in scripting some of his most vitriolic speeches.

One Trump characteristic had permanently endeared him to those wanting to roll the United States back to an earlier time when minorities knew they were blocked from certain aspects of the American dream before Barak Obama became President. Although he could not change history, Trump appeared to be determined to erase any accomplishments of the eight years of Barack Obama's Presidency. Trump supporters cheered when he reversed, rescinded or altered policies put in place by President Obama. Trump supporters even applauded when Trump reversed Obama policies that helped them personally in the past. When Trump attempted to repeal the Affordable Care Act and failed, he then proceeded to weaken the law and drove insurance costs up for those using the plan to provide for their medical care. Donald Trump also suspended a pay reporting requirement that was designed to assist in attacking the pay gap between men and women. The Presidency of Barack Obama was a low point in the history of White supremacists in the United States because it proved that members of a formerly ultimately oppressed group could reach the pinnacle of success in the United States, the Presidency.

Trump was powerless to erase the fact that Barack Obama was President for two terms, but he felt he could delete the legislative footprint Obama left on the United States. Of course, Trump asserted that Barack Obama was not born in the United States and therefore ineligible to be President when he led the birther movement. Trump seems to be obsessed with President Obama and took every opportunity to place blame for his own failings at the feet of Obama.

President Trump ushered in a new age of proud racism and it had real world negative effects for minorities across the country. Echoes of how Blacks faced baseless accusations of crimes from Whites during the days of Jim Crow seemed to have returned in force. Police officers were being used to terrorize minorities by some Whites calling in what they claimed were crimes in progress that often turned out to nothing more than non-Whites existing in their presence.

6

Many people in the United States had no idea about the Black Codes laws that were put in place in many states after slaves were freed following the Civil War. Black Codes varied by state and were almost a continuation of slavery because they restricted the rights of freed slaves. Some examples of Black Code restrictions were limits on owning property, gathering in groups and a Black person could be considered a vagrant without proof of work. There were also codes that forced freed slaves into indebtedness and forced labor. Showing papers to show proof of employment, residence etcetera were also included in some states Black Codes. Black codes existed during Reconstruction after the Civil War and effectively was just a new way to continue the practices of slavery. The Black Codes gave way to Jim Crow after Reconstruction ended in 1877. http://www.loc.gov/teachers/classroommaterials/primarysourcesets/civil-rights/pdf/teacher_guide.pdf

Jim Crow was not a single set of laws by consisted of various state and local laws, rules and practices that restricted the rights of African Americans and other minorities with the idea of forced segregation of the races. The United States seemed to have entered into a period of renewed Jim Crow combined with Black Code attitudes among some resentful White Americans who somehow felt compelled to report perceived minority violators of the law in their minds or in some cases direct confrontation.

There was a time during Jim Crow that baseless accusations against African Americans by a White person could and did result in the deaths of those accused. One of the most famous cases of a baseless or at least exaggerated accusation against a person of color that resulted in tragic consequences was what happened to 14 year old Emmitt Till. A White woman accused 14 year old Emmitt Till, who was from Chicago and visiting his uncle in Mississippi, of whistling at her when he entered a store she owned with her husband. Not only did the woman say that Till whistled at her, she also said he followed her behind the counter and grouped her while making lewd remarks totally out of character for a 14 year old boy. Till was kidnapped from his Uncle's house by the woman's husband and brother in law who tortured, shot and killed Emmitt Till. Till's body was tied to barbed connected to a cotton gin fan before being thrown into a river. Many decades later the woman reportedly admitted that much of what she said happened was a lie and Emmitt Till paid with his life. Till's murderers were acquitted by a jury of White men. Some may say what happened to Emmitt Till was during Jim Crow and doesn't happen anymore, but they would be wrong as a new outbreak of apparently racially motivated confrontations and malicious crime reports were initiated by some White individuals.

At Yale University a White female dorm resident called the police on a Black woman who fell asleep in a common room area of the dormitory with her study material around her indicating she was a student. Both the Black woman and White woman were students and lived in the dorm. The reason given by the White resident for calling the police was that sleeping was not allowed in the common room. Once the four officers arrived the black woman was placed in the position of having to prove she belonged there which resulted in a long period of wasted time, inconvenience and humiliation. The black student had to endure questioning about her identity, present official documents and wait for verification by the authorities which took longer because her name was spelled incorrectly in the University's database. Eventually the police were able to verify the right of the Black student to be in the dormitory where she lived and left the scene, but the damage was done. That incident was just one of what I call use of malicious official racial intimidation by way of crime reports to law enforcement targeting minorities for frivolous reasons. This incident could be called guilty of sleeping while Black.

Another incident of malicious racial intimidation occurred on the campus of Colorado

State University when a White woman with a group touring the campus as part of a group called 911 on two young men who joined the tour late. The Woman who called the authorities described the clothing, appearance and quiet demeanor of the duo. In her opinion the two young males appeared to be Hispanic and stated one of them said he was from Mexico when asked. The woman described their behavior as odd. Police arrived and questioned the suspected interlopers embedded within the campus tour group. Once again the accused were made to feel they had to justify their presence in a public space. The two individuals in question were Native American high school students who were brothers that took their lone family car and drove for hours to tour the Colorado State University campus as a potential place to go to college. Those two kids were guilty of touring a state university while being Native American. The call to the police from the woman that reported the two Native American brothers was simply due to her discomfort around people different from her.

Apparently, vacationing while Black was another potential criminal act in the eyes of some individuals. In California a group of black women were checking out of their rental property with their bags when the next door neighbor decided to call the police and reported they were stealing property from the home. Multiple police vehicles pulled up and reportedly a police helicopter flew overhead. Even after telling the officers they were leaving an AirBnB rental, they were not believed. The four women were finally allowed to go on their way, but you have to believe their vacation was ruined.

It is difficult enough to suffer the daily racial slights when living as a minority when doing simple things like shopping when suddenly noticing a store employee lurking around the corner pretending to straighten up items on display shelves as they kept an eye on you. The most recent incident I suffered was in a home improvement store while standing next to a display of outdoor lighting. I did have a question or two when a worker came down the aisle and turned the corner before I saw him. The store associate walked right past me like he was in a hurry, but then stopped about six feet from me and asked a middle aged White woman if she needed help. It was a strange feeling that left me questioning my visibility. A lot of thoughts can run through your mind over what seemed like a minor situation, such as would those companies rather not have minorities as customers. The other feeling was that some companies wanted your money, but did not want to put forth the effort to serve you as a person of color. It harkened back to the days when African Americans could eat in some restaurants, but only in the back out of sight of their White customers.

There were almost too many instances of the police being called for imaginary crimes by minorities to count by individuals, but companies were also getting in on the act. The problem with businesses is that they were run by humans who brought all their personal prejudices with them. One example of commercial entities as engaging in targeted racism was when two Black men, one with a valid membership and one with a four days pass were kicked out and had police called on them at a LA Fitness gymnasium in New Jersey. Apparently, upon investigation there was no other reason the men were kicked out other than they were working out while Black. The manager and two employees that worked at the club were fired over the incident. It seemed that working out while Black placed someone in jeopardy of being confronted by armed law enforcement officers.

Then there was the granddaddy of them all to that point and that was when two Black men were arrested in Philadelphia, Pennsylvania for using the restroom at a Starbucks® coffee shop without buying anything while they waited on a friend. The manager of the coffee shop called the police on two men who were doing what most people do at Starbucks®, nothing. Starbucks® promoted their locations as places to meet, hang out and use their free internet service. News of the incident at Starbucks® raced across the United States at lightning speed due to an age of seemingly everyone possessing handheld video recording devices on their persons embedded in cellular phones. Individuals witnessing the coffee shop arrests as they occurred stated they routinely did what the two Black men did without anyone working at the location raising an eyebrow. It seemed it took an incident at a coffee shop to demonstrate how blatant, everyday racism had crept back to the surface in the United States aided by permission slips passed out by the words of the President of the United States. Starbucks® realized the gravity of the blowback it was about to face and took the drastic step of closing all 8,000 locations for four hours for anti-racial bias training. Let it sink in for a moment that in the 21$^{st}$ century a major retail enterprise had to close its locations to train its employees to treat all customers the same regardless of their race, it was extraordinary. Using the bathroom while Black was added to a long list of actions worthy of a call to the police to report a crime.

The incidents continued to pile up and be mindful that for every instance that became public, there were many others that never saw the light of day. One troubling occurrence took place in Pennsylvania when a group of Black women golfers had the police called on them twice by a White man for allegedly playing too slow. When the 911 dispatcher asked if the women had any weapons, the complainant answered that the only weapon the women possessed was one member of the group's mouth. The women left the course and felt they were clearly singled out because of their race. The man who called the police not only used race as his reason to report the women, but fell back to another old racist trope that a Black person should not talk back to or disobey a White man's orders.

Outright lying on a Black man moving into his new apartment in New York was the basis of a call to the cops to report a Black man breaking into his own new apartment. A former White House staffer was moving into his new 5th floor apartment when uniformed officers showed up. The man was told a call came into dispatch stating that he used a long bar or tool to open the door of the apartment he was moving into that night. The man in question obviously had a key and the police left after a short period of time. Moving while Black subjected one to suspicion of committing a crime.

Possibly more dangerous than having the police called on someone because their race somehow made someone uncomfortable were the vigilante style interventions some engaged in like some kind of racist superheroes. The danger of an individual interjecting themselves into another person's space in a belligerent manner about something as sensitive as race has the potential for a violent reaction. A White man, who as it turned out was a lawyer, was caught on camera delivering a vile rant to a restaurant manager about lunch counter workers who were speaking Spanish to each other. The man demanded that the women should be speaking English because they were in America, but he did not stop there. The man accused the workers of being undocumented and in the United States illegally which he could rectify by calling the immigration service and have them kicked out of his country. All of the ugliness of traditional American racism leapt forth in the diatribe spewing out of the mouth of the man as he was engaged in an uncontrolled mind dump that included how he felt he was paying for the welfare of the Spanish speaking workers. The man paid the price because the video of his racist performance went viral online before crossing over to national news outlets and the backlash was swift. After his identity was exposed the lawyer was kicked out of his office space and even had a mariachi band sent to sing in Spanish outside his place of business.

The United States does not have an official language, but the man caught on camera was not alone in his anger stemming from thinking everyone in the nation should speak English. Interestingly enough, one of the workers that provoked the offended man's anger responded to him in English and called him a piece of shit as he walked away in words he could clearly understand.

Police have been called on a Black man working for a cable company while he surveyed a home for service installation and was checking for buried lines. He received a ticket despite having all of his work credentials and being dressed in company clothing. Working while Black was an activity that caused a report to law enforcement.

Police were called by a White woman to report a family in an Oakland, California park while they were barbequing at a location designated for that purpose. The woman stated to the cops that the family was using charcoal in an area specified for gas grilling although that provision was not strongly enforced. After the video of the incident went viral the complaining BBQ enforcer became an internet meme and in response the Black community in Oakland held a massive barbeque in the same park she was making the complaint about. Although the incident about the BBQ seemed trivial, it was actually the most offensive because it goes to the part of the Declaration of Independence dealing with enjoying the fruits of your equality and that was life, liberty and the pursuit of happiness. Nothing signifies enjoying your life, liberty and the pursuit of happiness more than spending time with your family at a cookout in the park, but this woman decided that particular Black family did not deserve that portion of the American experience because of her racism. She found the equivalence of the broken tail light pullover to ruin their day simply because she could. Enjoying your life, family and rewards of you labor while Black was perceived as a crime.

It was clear the fish was rotting from the head down in terms of racial hatred and intolerance, but what was responsible for an outbreak of racially motivated incidents across the United States?

7

Donald Trump served to supercharge existing racial tensions and animus among those in his base inclined to have distrust and ill feeling towards minorities, immigrants and others unlike them, but he went a step farther by mixing it with economic anxiety. Trump went into the heartland and rural areas of the United States and with his words provided fuel to the notion that the other was partially responsible for the economic downfall of the predominantly White populations in those locations. When Trump arrived on the scene as a Presidential candidate he was already carrying what some would have considered racially charged baggage from the past with housing discrimination lawsuits, advocating prison time for five Black and Latino youth after they were cleared by DNA of raping a White woman in Central Park in New York and of course advocating that President Barack Obama was not born in the United States. For a conventional politician entering a Presidential race with such controversial racial issues in his background would be almost unthinkable, but Trump did not view his past with racial issues as a liability, but as an asset.

Trump conducted a campaign based upon counterprogramming against the conventional politicians competing against him. Instead of attempting to overcome his historical racial issues, when combined with running as a Republican, would have been almost impossible if he tried to appeal to independents and moderate GOP voters. Trump went for those who would be inclined to be naturally attracted to his views on race along with others motivated to overlook them. Trump doubled, tripled and quadrupled down on his position as a racial and cultural warrior by adding immigrants and Muslims to his list of ills plaguing the United States. Instead of being a shining light to attract those seeking a higher purpose and vision of America, Trump became a black hole. Black holes pull in all matter and even light cannot escape the gravitational force and Trump became a political black hole. Trump pulled in those White voters with negative energy towards those different than they were, those with negative job prospects and economic outlooks for the future of all races along with those weary of the current politics because nothing positive had occurred in their lives from voting for them over the years. Those Whites that felt over the years they had been diminished in social stature by the rise of minorities and immigrants happily went into candidate Trump's black hole. Trump energized a group of people that felt they had been overlooked, disrespected and mischaracterized by the media on both coasts and forgotten by politicians in Washington DC too focused on their special interests. Trump won with an interesting coalition of the desperate, party loyalists and the angry.

With promises to revive the coal industry, bring prosperity back to areas ravaged by industrial job losses and recriminations against illegal immigrants inside or attempting to enter the United States allowed Trump to squeak out a victory of about 70,000 votes in Michigan, Pennsylvania and Wisconsin to win the Presidency in the Electoral College. Although he lost the popular vote by about three million, it did not matter, but it did contribute to turbulence in the nation, because Trump only seemed to care about those who voted for him. The truth is that Donald Trump would have never become President if prior political leaders had been candid with those left behind about how the world of work was changing so they could have been prepared. Blue collar workers were allowed to continue to show up for work until automation, globalized production or new technology eliminated the jobs they depended on to support their families.

Instead of manufacturing, mining and other industrial workers preparing themselves and their offspring to continue to be vital cogs in a new economy, they were allowed to become obsolete. The loss of viable work for non-college educated workers accustomed to earning a wage that once placed them solidly in the middle class left a vacuum of despair than grew deeper as the years passed. As those in the financial, technological and healthcare sectors prospered, many of those in declining fields like manufacturing suffered while machines and lower cost of labor in other countries separated them from their once dependable paychecks. Donald Trump stepped into the vacuum of despair that existed in the heartland of the United States and told them he alone could fix it.

Those who voted for Trump thought they had a lifeline to hang onto to help improve their economic conditions that had been eroding for decades. Those in government had ample notice that structural changes in the job market were coming because it was projected for years by the federal agency that tracked and predicted shifts in the employment structure of the United States. The following excerpt from the Occupational Outlook Quarterly Spring 2003 examined employment projections from the years of 1988 through 2000 for accuracy. Many of the occupations slated for decline were rooted in the industrial sectors of the nation that Trump targeted during the 2016 Presidential election. That 2003 report clearly showed that thirty years ago the writing was on the wall for a dramatic shift in the United States when it came to employment. Thirty years was longer than a generation and there should have been transition planning not only for the workers, but for the regions as well. Information from the Occupational Outlook Quarterly Spring 2003 is below:

Declining occupations

Just as the basic assumptions were accurate for fast-growing occupations, assumptions also were accurate for occupational declines. For example, of the projected 20 fastest declining occupations, more than half actually declined, with 7 of the occupations among the fastest declining. And like those of fast-growing occupations, projections of declining occupations were conservative. Rates of decline in most occupations were much higher than projected.

Unlike the varied reasons for differences between actual and projected fast-growth occupations, however, one reason stands out in comparing actual with projected declines: the underestimated effects of technological advance on employment. The decline in employment of railroad brake, signal, and switch operators, for example, was more rapid than projected because of an increased us of computer-controlled train cars. These cars operate the brakes, doors, alert systems, and signals automatically, thus reducing the number of workers needed to operate a train.

Gains in technology also were responsible for fast employment declines in textile occupations, such as garment sewing machine operators and precision shoe and leather workers and repairers. Other groups of occupations with fast declines in employment because of technology include some administrative support workers—such as word processors and typists—and machinery assemblers, installers, and repairers—such as precision aircraft assemblers.

Unexpected changes in technology affected occupations in ways that could not be anticipated at the time the projections were made. In many cases, new technology caused employment declines in occupations that were projected to grow. During the 1990s, the most significant technological advance was the Internet, from which emerged electronic commerce, or e-commerce. The Internet and e-commerce allow consumers to research and purchase an assortment of goods and services directly from suppliers, thereby reducing the need for buyers and sales agents to act as go-betweens. One group of occupations whose employment was adversely affected by the Internet was sales occupations, specifically wholesale and retail buyers, except farm products; purchasing managers; insurance sales agents; real estate sales agents; and travel agents. https://www.bls.gov/careeroutlook/2003/spring/art01.pdf

The following was the conclusion from the Bureau of Labor Statistics as to the accuracy of the 1988 through 2000 employment projections:

Final analysis:

74

As past evaluations have shown, BLS occupational projections tend toward conservatism. Projected employment for the largest number of occupations was concentrated in the average growth range, whereas most actually grew faster or declined. Employment in occupations projected to have the most rapid employment growth was underestimated, and occupations projected to experience little growth or to decline experienced greater declines than anticipated.

https://www.bls.gov/careeroutlook/2003/spring/art01.pdf

Based upon the conclusions from the 2003 report on occupational changes between 1988 and 2000, the decline of manufacturing, retail and administrative support workers largely due to technology advances was steeper than projected and it should be no surprise that job prospects became even more grim almost two decades later. If the slide in industrial blue collar employment was already on the decline in 2000, the question thirty years later was, where did the high earning opportunities go and who could get them. The following report from the U.S. Bureau of Labor Statistics gave us answers to those questions:

# Fastest growing occupations

Other available formats: (XLSx)

Table 1.3 Fastest growing occupations, 2016 and projected 2026
(Numbers in thousands)

| 2016 National Employment Matrix title and code | | Employment | | Change, 2016–26 | | Median annual wage, 2017[1] |
|---|---|---|---|---|---|---|
| | | 2016 | 2026 | Number | Percent | |
| Total, all occupations | 00-0000 | 156,063.8 | 167,582.3 | 11,518.6 | 7.4 | $37,690 |
| Solar photovoltaic installers | 47-2231 | 11.3 | 23.1 | 11.8 | 104.9 | $39,490 |
| Wind turbine service technicians | 49-9081 | 5.8 | 11.3 | 5.6 | 96.3 | $53,880 |
| Home health aides | 31-1011 | 911.5 | 1,342.7 | 431.2 | 47.3 | $23,210 |
| Personal care aides | 39-9021 | 2,016.1 | 2,793.8 | 777.6 | 38.6 | $23,100 |
| Physician assistants | 29-1071 | 106.2 | 145.9 | 39.6 | 37.3 | $104,860 |
| Nurse practitioners | 29-1171 | 155.5 | 211.6 | 56.1 | 36.1 | $103,880 |
| Statisticians | 15-2041 | 37.2 | 49.8 | 12.6 | 33.8 | $84,060 |
| Physical therapist assistants | 31-2021 | 88.3 | 115.8 | 27.4 | 31.0 | $57,430 |
| Software developers, applications | 15-1132 | 831.3 | 1,086.6 | 255.4 | 30.7 | $101,790 |
| Mathematicians | 15-2021 | 3.1 | 4.0 | 0.9 | 29.7 | $103,010 |
| Physical therapist aides | 31-2022 | 52.0 | 67.2 | 15.3 | 29.4 | $25,730 |
| Bicycle repairers | 49-3091 | 12.4 | 16.1 | 3.6 | 29.3 | $28,390 |
| Medical assistants | 31-9092 | 634.4 | 818.4 | 183.9 | 29.0 | $32,480 |
| Genetic counselors | 29-9092 | 3.1 | 4.0 | 0.9 | 29.0 | $77,480 |
| Occupational therapy assistants | 31-2011 | 39.3 | 50.7 | 11.4 | 28.9 | $59,310 |
| Information security analysts | 15-1122 | 100.0 | 128.5 | 28.5 | 28.5 | $95,510 |
| Physical therapists | 29-1123 | 239.8 | 306.9 | 67.1 | 28.0 | $86,850 |
| Operations research analysts | 15-2031 | 114.0 | 145.3 | 31.3 | 27.4 | $81,390 |
| Forest fire inspectors and prevention specialists | 33-2022 | 1.7 | 2.2 | 0.5 | 26.6 | $37,380 |
| Massage therapists | 31-9011 | 160.3 | 202.4 | 42.1 | 26.3 | $39,990 |
| Health specialties teachers, postsecondary | 25-1071 | 233.5 | 294.0 | 60.6 | 25.9 | $97,870 |
| Derrick operators, oil and gas | 47-5011 | 11.1 | 13.9 | 2.8 | 25.7 | $46,140 |
| Roustabouts, oil and gas | 47-5071 | 50.0 | 62.4 | 12.4 | 24.8 | $36,960 |
| Occupational therapy aides | 31-2012 | 7.5 | 9.3 | 1.8 | 24.7 | $29,200 |
| Phlebotomists | 31-9097 | 122.7 | 152.8 | 30.1 | 24.5 | $33,670 |
| Nonfarm animal caretakers | 39-2021 | 241.5 | 300.0 | 58.5 | 24.2 | $22,950 |
| Rotary drill operators, oil and gas | 47-5012 | 16.7 | 20.8 | 4.0 | 24.2 | $53,980 |
| Nursing instructors and teachers, postsecondary | 25-1072 | 67.9 | 84.2 | 16.3 | 24.0 | $71,260 |

Footnotes:
(1) Data are from the Occupational Employment Statistics program, U.S. Bureau of Labor Statistics. Wage data cover non-farm wage and salary workers and do not cover the self-employed, owners and partners in unincorporated firms, or household workers.
Source: Employment Projections program, U.S. Bureau of Labor Statistics

| 2016 National Employment Matrix title and code | | Employment | | Change, 2016–26 | | Median annual wage, 2017[1] |
|---|---|---|---|---|---|---|
| | | 2016 | 2026 | Number | Percent | |
| Occupational therapists | 29-1122 | 130.4 | 161.4 | 31.0 | 23.8 | $83,200 |
| Service unit operators, oil, gas, and mining | 47-5013 | 41.4 | 51.1 | 9.7 | 23.4 | $48,290 |

Footnotes:
  [1] Data are from the Occupational Employment Statistics program, U.S. Bureau of Labor Statistics. Wage data cover non-farm wage and salary workers and do not cover the self-employed, owners and partners in unincorporated firms, or household workers.
  Source: Employment Projections program, U.S. Bureau of Labor Statistics

https://www.bls.gov/emp/tables/fastest-growing-occupations.htm

After reviewing the occupations on the chart with sizable employment and compensation from $80,000 to above $100,000, we discover they were clustered in the areas of healthcare and computer technology that required specialized education or college degrees. To emphasize a point the number of people employed as software developers was listed at over 830,000 individuals earning over $100,000 per year compared to just over 41,000 combined working in the Service unit operators, oil, gas, and mining sectors earning about $48,000 per year. Software development employment was projected to increase to over one million by 2026.

While it was clear from the objective data compiled over the years that job relocation played a part in blue collar job declines, the primary driver appears to be from the impact of technology. Industrial robots have displaced millions of factory workers by taking over repetitive tasks previously performed by people. Automation has replaced humans in a wide variety of industries.

- Online retailers caused job losses and retail location closures
- Automated telephone technology service decreased the need for human customer service workers
- Electronic communications reduced the need for mail delivery workers
- Automated product assembly reduced the number of factory workers and locations required to meet production goals
- Automated warehouse technology reduced the number of workers needed to handle the same amount of item movement

With information available that clearly stated automation was responsible for huge blue collar job losses, Trump focused on trade policies, job relocation to foreign countries and immigrants as the reasons for blue collar job losses.

Trump parked on the immigrant issue in order to thoroughly demonize them. The United States was a nation of immigrants except for Native Americans. Trump railed against immigrants from Mexico from the first moments of his campaign until Election Day. Trump's promise to build a southern border wall to keep Mexicans from illegally crossing the border into the United States, that he said Mexico would pay for, was his biggest response line at his rallies. The demonstration of Trump's commitment to keep illegal immigrants out of the United States was the episode of migrant children being separated from their parents and confined to internment centers that sparked outrage among many and elicited shrugged shoulders from some.

Trump's immigrant bashing campaign allowed individuals to pick their poison when it came to their negative impact on jobs formerly held by them, if so inclined. Those who had witnessed their jobs being shipped off to Mexico or other countries really could not blame immigrants because the management of their employers made the decision to relocate the operation to another country entirely. Those whose prior work locations were shuttered because increased production efficiency due to automation allowed consolidation of work into fewer physical locations within the United States knew their job loss was not due to immigrants displacing them. Those jobs that were being done by H1B visa holders with specialized skills were not on the radar of underemployed industrial workers because they did not have the skill sets required. By and large the group Trump was targeting was doing work most American citizens shunned because of the level of compensation. Many immigrants worked low wage jobs that required little in the way of formal education.

If Trump's characterization of the impact of immigrants on industrial jobs was a red herring, then what was his real intent? Trump's intent with his constant immigrant basing was distraction through hate and division. Those predisposed to dislike immigrants and especially brown immigrants from Mexico and farther south had a kindred spirit running for President who became more valuable as President of the United States. As far as the public was concerned it was a hatefest gone live that continued after Trump's election. Hispanics were not the only targeted immigrant group.

Muslims were on the list for Trump's scorn and used to instill fear. Trump capitalized upon a terrible mass shooting in California by promising to institute a Muslim immigration ban if he was elected. Reports of Muslim women being targeted because they wore hijabs were logged. In May of 2017, two men were stabbed to death while attempting to protect two young Muslim women on a light rail train in Oregon from a man harassing them.

Multiple reports of Hispanic students of all ages being told by their classmates that they would be deported now that Trump was President began to be reported. The public did not simply sit back and accept the harsher tone of intolerance in the United States without a response.

There was an aggressive push back from citizens to the hate and division that was being ushered in after the election of the 45th President of the United States. Massive anti-Trump protests occurred starting on the day after he was inaugurated. The largest anti-Trump march was a worldwide Women's march to advocate for the rights of women of all kind to be able to live their lives without intrusive interference from outside forces, but some loved Trump's vitriol.

The same speeches that terrified Hispanics, Muslims and belittled African Americans earned candidate Trump an endorsement from the official newspaper of the Ku Klux Klan before the election. Shouts of Hail Trump came from an alt-right leader at gathering held Saturday November 19, 2016 after his election victory complete with Nazi salutes from the attendees. The pro-Trump alt-right activity was captured on video and later broadcast nationwide on social media and national television news networks. Once the activity that occurred at the alt-right conference became public, the Trump transition team issued a statement in response:

"President-elect Trump has continued to denounce racism of any kind and he was elected because he will be a leader for every American,"

"To think otherwise is a complete misrepresentation of the movement that united Americans from all backgrounds." read a statement released by his transition team.

Given the tepid nature of the Trump Transition Team's response to endorsement from racial hate groups shortly after his election, in hindsight, it was logical to expect a disaster like the alt-Right clash in Charlottesville, Virginia to be just a matter of time to occur. Trump's Transition Team failed to condemn the alt-Right in November of 2016 just as he cast blame on many sides after the calamity in Charlottesville. It must be noted that one of Trump's top advisors was Steve Bannon, one of the founders of Brietbart News Network that Bannon once said he wanted to be the platform for the alt-Right. It was not difficult to imagine how Trump would have a difficult time denouncing the alt-Right, neo-Nazis and Ku Klux Klan when he had an alt-Right enabler at his side. At one point Bannon was blamed for the way Trump approached issues of race, but after Bannon's departure from the White House in the midst of the uproar over how the President responded to Charlottesville nothing changed about how he handled issues of race. Trump made his incendiary comments about professional football players protesting about police treatment of minorities and insulting comments about Puerto Ricans after a disastrous hurricane struck the island after Bannon left the administration. It was then that it was clear that the President was, and had always been, someone that had a history of racially radioactive episodes in his background.

Trump was not being led down a racist path, but was blazing a racist trail. Trump's pardoning of Arizona Sheriff Joe Arpaio who the U.S. Department of Justice found oversaw a department that committed the worst case of racial profiling in the history of the United States shocked everyone. Arpaio was found guilty of disobeying a court order to cease racial profiling by detaining individuals suspected of being in the United States illegally. An excerpt of the U.S. Department of Justice findings after an investigation into Sherriff Joe Arpaio and the Maricopa County Sheriff's Department is below:

FACTUAL FINDINGS

We find that MCSO deputies, detention officers, supervisory staff, and command staff, including Sheriff Arpaio, have engaged in a widespread pattern or practice of law enforcement and jail activities that discriminate against Latinos. This discrimination flows directly from a culture of bias and institutional deficiencies that result in the discriminatory treatment of Latinos.

https://www.justice.gov/sites/default/files/crt/legacy/2011/12/15/mcso_findlett er_12-15-11.pdf

In line with Trump's constant drumbeat against Hispanic immigrants in general, he found a way to punctuate his credentials with those who were chanting build the wall during the Presidential campaign. Trump used his Presidential pardon powers to pardon Sherriff Joe Arpaio. What better way for President Trump to demonstrated to the racist portion of his base how he felt about protecting the civil rights of all Americans than by pardoning the nation greatest practitioner of official racial profiling? Trump's pardon for Arpaio is below:

# DONALD J. TRUMP

## *President of the United States of America*

TO ALL TO WHOM THESE PRESENTS SHALL COME, GREETING:

BE IT KNOWN, THAT THIS DAY, I, DONALD J. TRUMP, PRESIDENT OF THE UNITED STATES, PURSUANT TO MY POWERS UNDER ARTICLE II, SECTION 2, CLAUSE 1, OF THE CONSTITUTION, HAVE GRANTED UNTO

### JOSEPH M. ARPAIO

### A FULL AND UNCONDITIONAL PARDON

FOR HIS CONVICTION of Section 401(3), Title 18, United States Code (Docket No. 2.16-CR-01012-SRB) in the United States District Court for the District of Arizona, of which he was convicted on July 31, 2017, and for which sentencing is currently set for October 5, 2017; and

FOR ANY OTHER OFFENSES under Chapter 21 of Title 18, United States Code that might arise, or be charged, in connection with *Melendres v. Arpaio* (Docket No. 2:07-CV-02513-GMS) in the United States District Court for the District of Arizona.

IN TESTIMONY WHEREOF, I have hereunto signed my name and caused the seal of the Department of Justice to be affixed.

*Done at the City of Washington this twenty-fifth day of August, in the year of our Lord two thousand and seventeen and of the Independence of the United States of America the two hundred and forty-second.*

DONALD J. TRUMP
PRESIDENT

The pardoning of Joe Arpaio could be viewed as a act of White reparations being paid. Arpaio was convicted of overseeing a taxpayer funded racial profiling machine against Hispanics. The fact that the President of the United States would pardon Arpaio had to be incredibly satisfying for those supporting his actions against Hispanics. After his pardon Arpaio launched a campaign for the U.S. Senate and said he would renew his efforts to prove President Barack Obama's birth certificate was not authentic.

Emboldened by a new sense of freedom to speak their minds on racial matters, multiple White Nationalists threw their hat into the ring to run for public office nationwide. In the year 2018 White supremacists were so normalized that they considered running for public office to be perfectly acceptable to the public at large.

8

The United States was thrust into an all out culture war on issues of race, gender and class, seemingly at will, since it elected a President who focused on dividing the nation on multiple fronts. Was there a desire to introduce cultural unrest into United States society or did the voting public misjudge the degree of latent racial, gender and class bias present within the general public. For all the talk of a post-racial society after Barack Obama's election, the United States seemed more racially divided than ever, but in reality it was an intentional exacerbation of racial animus that existed within a minority of individuals throughout the nation.

Many of the headline grabbing racial controversies did not occur of an organic nature, but were engineered by racially provocative statements from positions of high authority that resulted in predictable backlash. One such occurrence was the backlash from the President referring to professional football players as sons of bitches that should be fired if they did not stand for the national anthem as a show of patriotism. President Trump made his sons of bitches comment on September 2017 and in June 2018 he cancelled a visit to the White House by the National Football League® champion winning team, the Philadelphia Eagles® due to a low number of players agreeing to attend due to their views about the kneeling protests that Trump attacked. Some expressed outrage that the team would pass on the tradition of national championship sports teams visiting the White House, but that outrage was a pretense at best.

Trump's profane reference about protesting football players was assumed to be aimed at predominately African Americans. That very few players would want to attend an event hosted by a man, President or not, who called them sons of bitches and lied about why they were kneeling before the start of games should not have surprised anyone. For African American men to stand smiling next to a man that insulted them in a most vile and personal way would conjure up memories when African Americans suffered all manner of insults, rapes and abuse from slave owners, employers etc. without the ability to protest because they were in bondage during slavery or in dire need to maintain employment after slavery. The idea of seeing proud young Black men standing around a smiling Donald Trump with knowledge of the insult he delivered previously would have been disheartening to African Americans and others, but those with certain points of view about racial hierarchy would have drawn great comfort from such an image. An image of wealthy young black men posing with a President who insulted them would have been used in an age of social media for racist propaganda purposes.

The uproar over immigrants that came from shithole countries, Puerto Ricans wanting everything done for them and using Pocahontas as a slur in front of Navajo code talkers were all created out of thin air by President Donald Trump. Many of the most controversial flashpoints regarding racial and cultural issues roiling the nation appeared to be intentionally ignited from the highest seats of power in the United States government which should be a cause for great concern for the nation.

The noise, furor and concern over the cultural struggle taking place in the United States should not be ignored or overblown, but it has to be met head own without regard to political party or deference to titles. What was even more dangerous than the obvious outward social concerns created by the ugly underbelly of cultural bias being brought to the surface was that it was done so with the power of law behind it. More aggressive immigration enforcement, harsher sentencing guidelines for federal crimes and more restrictive abortion laws were implemented in several states.

As mentioned previously, sexism was on full display across the nation and many women pushed back, but some women were caught between allegiance to their race or their gander. Black women seemed to deal with their gender issues inside their race. Since Black women would always be perceived as Black by the wider world it became a given that they had to deal with their gender issues as a Black person who also had to grapple with issues they struggled with as women. White women knew they had gender equality issues to deal with, but many chose to approach race from the standpoint of being White. Donald Trump won a majority of White women voters during the 2016 Presidential election despite ample evidence that he did not view women as equally created. Before the election candidate Trump had a prior hot microphone recording broadcast nationwide that revealed exactly how he felt about women:

Trump was recorded on a live microphone moment with an entertainment show host, recounting how he attempted to have sex with a married woman while married to his new wife, Melania.

Trump said in crude terms, "I did try and fuck her. She was married …," along with other statements about the episode, but it was something else he said while being recorded that set off a firestorm.

"When you're a star, they let you do it. You can do anything," Trump said.

When asked to what extent he meant.

"Grab them by the pussy. You can do anything," Trump said.

Trump was fifty-nine years old at the time of the recording. There was no question it was Trump who said those things because the audio was contained in a video recorded when he was on a bus that transported him to a soap opera television show taping. Video of the bus pulling up, parking and Trump stepping off the vehicle left no doubt that he was the one who was speaking. Over one dozen women came out and accused Trump of sexual harassment or sexual assault after the broadcast of his sexist admissions.

The prevailing thought was that no candidate for President could survive something like the release of the misogynistic recordings of Donald Trump relating his thoughts and actions regarding women, more women voted for Trump than his opponent who was a woman. Estimates were that over 50% of White women voted for Donald Trump and could be the reason he was elected. Many asked why so many women would vote for a man who treated and thought about women the way he did. It appeared that White women voted for the same reasons as White men with political party affiliation, wanting good jobs to come back and some White women harbored views that they also have been marginalized by the rise of others in the United States. It was a fair bet that those White men overheard sharing their frustrations at not being on top of the heap anymore were married to White women that shared their sentiments. In addition to women who voted for Trump for a host of economic and political reasons, there was a group of angry White women out there that wanted things made great again also. The fact that Trump said how he felt about women was something women that voted for Trump overlooked because, in their minds, he wasn't talking about them. The odds that women voting for Trump would be within range for him to grab them by the genitals or start kissing them was almost zero, so they voted for their preferred  candidate for other reasons like jobs or attraction to his racist agenda.

Race, gender and politics had always been complicated because it was never clear which factor pushed or repelled a voter to or from a candidate running for office. There had always been the clash of Women's rights overall versus Women's rights within their racial or religious groups and there was a big difference. The prime example of when race and gender separated in the United States was the 19th amendment to the Constitution of the United States that granted the right to vote regardless of the sex of the voter that was ratified by Congress on August 18, 1920.

# Sixty-sixth Congress of the United States of America;

## At the First Session,

Begun and held at the City of Washington on Monday, the nineteenth day of May, one thousand nine hundred and nineteen.

---

## JOINT RESOLUTION

Proposing an amendment to the Constitution extending the right of suffrage to women.

---

*Resolved by the Senate and House of Representatives of the United States of America in Congress assembled (two-thirds of each House concurring therein),* That the following article is proposed as an amendment to the Constitution, which shall be valid to all intents and purposes as part of the Constitution when ratified by the legislatures of three-fourths of the several States.

"ARTICLE ————.

"The right of citizens of the United States to vote shall not be denied or abridged by the United States or by any State on account of sex.

"Congress shall have power to enforce this article by appropriate legislation."

*Speaker of the House of Representatives.*

*Vice President of the United States and President of the Senate.*

93

Like most rights granted in the United States, the right for women to be able to vote nationally was hard fought and came after a prolonged struggle. While women could vote nationally due to the 19th amendment, in the south, Black women were constrained from voting by Jim Crow laws, poll taxes and various other impediments at the polls. In the case of women's right to vote Black women had their right to vote restricted in the south due to their race over gender. There were myriad racial and gender issues surrounding the granting of the right to vote. The 15th amendment was ratified February 3, 1870 and granted all men the right to vote regardless of race, but did not grant the right to vote regardless of sex. Black men gained the right to vote via the 15th amendment, but White women did not and some were incensed at having Black men elevated over them in that manner.

15th Amendment to the Constitution of the United States

The right of citizens of the United States to vote shall not be denied or abridged by the United States or by any State on account of race, color, or previous condition of servitude.

The Congress shall have power to enforce this article by appropriate legislation.

Ryan-Hitch-
cock mode of
marine fortifica-
tions to be in-
quired into, and
report made to
Congress.

the admiral of the navy, or in the absence of the admiral, then the vice-admiral, be authorized and directed to inquire into the utility and practicability of the Ryan-Hitchcock mode of marine fortifications, and that they report to Congress at the next session thereof.

APPROVED, February 19, 1869.

---

Feb. 27, 1869.    [No. 14.] *A Resolution proposing an Amendment to the Constitution of the United States.*

Fifteenth
amendment to
the Constitution.

*Resolved by the Senate and House of Representatives of the United States of America in Congress assembled,* (*two thirds of both houses concurring,*) That the following article be proposed to the legislatures of the several States as an amendment to the Constitution of the United States, which, when ratified by three fourths of said legislatures, shall be valid as part of the Constitution, namely:

### ARTICLE XV.

SECTION 1. The right of citizens of the United States to vote shall not be denied or abridged by the United States or by any State on account of race, color, or previous condition of servitude.

SEC. 2. The Congress shall have power to enforce this article by appropriate legislation.

SCHUYLER COLFAX,
*Speaker of the House of Representatives.*
B. F. WADE,
*President of the Senate pro tempore.*

Attest:
EDWD. McPHERSON,
*Clerk of House of Representatives.*
GEO. C. GORHAM,
*Sec'y of Senate U. S.*

Received at Department of State February 27, 1869.

---

March 1, 1869.
——
1864, ch. 217,
§ 10.
Vol. xiii. p. 370.

[No. 15.] *Joint Resolution gr[a]n[t]i[n]g the Consent of Congress provided for in section ten of the Act incorporating the Northern Pacific Railroad Company, approved July second, eighteen hundred and sixty-four.*

Consent of
Congress given
to the Northern
Pacific R. R. Co.
to issue bonds,
&c.

*Be it resolved by the Senate and House of Representatives of the United States of America in Congress assembled,* That the consent of the Congress of the United States is hereby given to the Northern Pacific Railroad Company to issue its bonds, and to secure the same by mortgage upon its railroad and its telegraph line, for the purpose of raising funds with which to construct said railroad and telegraph line between Lake Superior and Puget Sound, and also upon its branch to a point at or near Portland, Oregon; and the term "Puget Sound," as used here and in the act incorporating said company, is hereby construed to mean all the waters connected with the straits of Juan de Fuca within the territory of the United States.

APPROVED, March 1, 1869.

---

March 1, 1869.    [No. 16.] *Joint Resolution in Relation to the Meeting of the House of Representatives at the first Session of the Forty-first Congress.*

Time of first
regular meeting
of the House of
Representatives
of the 41st
Congress.

*Be it resolved by the Senate and House of Representatives of the United States of America in Congress assembled,* That the time for the first regular meeting of the House of Representatives of the Forty-first Congress be, and is hereby, postponed from twelve o'clock meridian, on the fourth day of March, eighteen hundred and sixty-nine, to the hour of three o'clock in the afternoon of the said day.

APPROVED, March 1, 1869.

---

While Black men gained the right to vote, attempting to exercise it was deadly to many. Thousands of Black men were lynched after attempting to register to vote after their right to do so was granted by law. The women's suffrage movement to gain the right to vote was laced with racist hate against Black men and some resentment toward Black women because White men had sex with them during slavery. Anna Howard Shaw, a leader in the Women's right to vote movement, stated, "You have put the ballot in the hands of your black men, thus making them political superiors of white women. Never before in the history of the world have men made former slaves the political masters of their former mistresses!" Seething resentment aimed at Black women for the behavior of White men during slavery when Black women had no option to resist the sexual advances of their masters is shocking when viewed in the 21$^{st}$ century.

Black men also faced characterizations relating to their right to vote as drunken sexual monsters trading their votes for liquor. Rebecca Latimer Felton the first woman U.S Senator said in 1897, years before she was appointed to the Senate, "if it takes lynching to protect women's dearest possession from drunken, ravening human beasts, then I say lynch a thousand a week."

Due to racial animosity, the mainstream women's right to vote movement excluded Black, Asian and Native American women. The realization that Women rights had been advancing along separate racial tracks appeared to come into the nation's consciousness near the end of the 20th century. In the 21st century a new movement called Me Too was started by a Black woman, Tarana Burke, in 2006 to focus on empowering women of color who had suffered sexual assault. In 2017 the Me Too movement went global as high profile Hollywood stars began relating their stories of unwanted sexual advances and sexual assaults at the hands of powerful men in the entertainment industry. The adoption of the Me Too movement was one of the largest if not the largest instance of White women embracing in mass an effort pioneered by a Black woman.

There was a very complex and layered mix of race, gender issues and even resentment involved in how women's right issues were advanced in the United States. It was ironic that women of all races bonded together in the Me Too movement that was started by a Black woman. There was no such thing as a Me Too movement for women in slavery to rally around and report unwanted sexual assaults.

There were plenty of angry White women wanting America made great again and they voted for the man they thought could make it happen. By reviewing some of the most reported incidents of Whites using the police as instruments of racial intimidation, many of those initiating those calls to law enforcement were White women. White women made the calls to law enforcement in the barbequing, sleeping and vacationing while Black encounters with uniformed officers.

All was not lost because the largest anti-Trump protest was a worldwide march of women pushing back against misogyny and fighting against policies restricting the rights of women. College educated women began to pull away from continuing to support an administration that rolled back some measures relating to the ability of women to report pay disparities with men. Trump reversed some women's equal pay measures implemented by President Obama. One item suspended by Trump required employers to report information about their employees' pay by race, age, gender and ethnicity. Trump stated it was too burdensome for companies to be required to report that information to the government. Due to Trump's pullback from rules designed to make it easier to spot gender based discrimination and his increased entanglement in multiple legal actions due to women suing him over sexual harassment, past extramarital relationships and hush money payoffs many women began to withdraw their support.

Trump maintained his most fervent supporters who were not shaken by anything he said or did. Some women responded with the same robustness as men to Trump's attacks on professional football players for not standing during the national anthem as being unpatriotic. Obviously women in a family unit often harbored similar sentiments as their male partners, even when it came to race, but the angry White woman was not cited as a distinct group nearly as much as the angry White man, however they were out there.

It was evident from some of the statements expressed by prominent White women after slavery that they held profoundly racist views and allowed those feelings to guide their actions as they fought for equality. During slavery the White women in slave owning households were there, just like the men, participating in a system where one group of humans subjugated other humans to the status of property based upon their race. Complicit by their presence during slavery, the Civil War and Jim Crow, there was no reason not to expect some White women would harbor the same feelings of White supremacy as some White men.

Possibly a watershed cultural moment occurred that left no doubt about the depth of racial hate that could come from a White woman occurred was a tweet sent out by comedian/actress Roseanne Barr in the early morning on June 29, 2019. Barr was someone with a lot to lose having recently launched a wildly successful new version of her situation comedy show that previously ended in 1997. The tweet sent out by Barr was short, devastating and conjured up some of the ugliest and most despicable memories of racial hatred in the history of the United States. Barr tweeted:

"muslim brotherhood & planet of the apes had a baby = vj"

VJ in Barr's tweet referred to Valerie Jarrett, advisor to former President Barack Obama. Barr's tweet managed to smear Muslims and African Americans with a few carefully chosen words. The aspect of the tweet that was so repulsive related to referring to an African American as an ape. Dehumanization of Africans and African American by Whites by calling them apes, monkeys or animals was deeply ingrained in the history of the United States. Dehumanization of a group of people makes it easier to treat them in inhumane ways as was done during slavery. Reaction to Roseanne's unprovoked racist attack was swift as her highly rated and highly rated show was cancelled. The widespread public revulsion to Roseanne's Twitter attack on a high profile African American woman demonstrated that the seemingly pervasive explosion of racial backlash and psychological reparation collection by aggrieved White Americans was smaller, concentrated and magnified by exposure. Roseanne Barr was an example of a high profile individual launching a racial attack that raced around the world, but Barr would be fine because she was famous and wealthy, but others made the same mistake and sent their lives into turmoil.

A group of friends were driving on an unpaved road at night in Missouri when a male voice behind the camera said, "Hey, so we going nigger hunting today or what?! We're fucking nigger hunting right now, huh?!"

"You get them niggers," a barefoot young White woman replied while sitting on the top of a vehicle.

The video of the brief racist outburst was posted on the social media page of a female friend of the 20 year old woman who made her racist statement with her face in full view of the camera. The racist video went viral and complaints came in to the young woman's employer which prompted them to fire from her job as a waitress. The racist uttering from the young woman supposedly on a nigger hunt also got her kicked out of the Air Force after she had recently enlisted. Unlike Roseanne Barr, the woman in the video most likely did not have fame or wealth to cushion her fall and only managed to complicate her life and future for a brief racist eruption.

In a nation with hundreds of millions of potential citizen reporters able to capture almost anything that occurs between individuals in a group setting, we are presented with many racist encounters on almost a daily basis. Coffee shops, grocery store checkout lines and lunch counter racial incidents were routinely circulating on social media. To be clear, racists were openly expressing their first amendment rights by releasing their pent up resentments in full public view. Often after public exposure and backlash from their fellow citizens, those who though their retrograde views on race were shared by the public at large attempted to retract their passionately expressed sentiments that played well in their like minded social circles. Jobs were lost, relationships were frayed and social standings destroyed by some who decided it was fashionable to publically assail others based up their feelings of White superiority if it was caught on camera.

The bottom line was that many of the individuals that bought into the illusion that America would be made great again missed one crucial element of the message. The intent was to make America great again, but not for them and not in the way they imagined, but there was a crucial role for them to play.

9


One has to go back to the original United States Constitution to determine who was meant to benefit from America being made great again and what time in United States history was the model for that revived greatness. Some assumed they were automatically included among those the new age of prominence was meant for due to their race, racial views or cultural stance. Anti-minority, anti-immigrant and anti-Muslim attitudes were erroneously interpreted to be the admission ticket to enjoy the restored socioeconomic positions they would occupy as others were pushed to the back of the line for their benefit, but they missed the point.

Those among us who felt liberated to openly share their disdain for whatever race, religion or sexual orientation they chose did so with relish, but did not realize that alone would be their reward. To bring clarity to the situation we had to examine what really mattered in the United States and that was who held power and who was entitled to have a voice in selecting who could hold that power. It all went back to the ability to vote. As improbable as it seemed, the U.S. Constitution does not guarantee the right to vote and never did. The Constitution through amendments outlined what cannot be used to prevent individuals from voting such as race and sex, but does not state anyone had a right to vote.

When the United States was formed voting rights was a state by state issue and in most cases was restricted to White men who owned property. In today's world non-property owners can vote in every state. Imagine the outrage if renters or voting age eligible young adults still living at home could not vote because they were not property owners in today's America. There was no way for the United States to be taken back to a time when the right to vote was restricted to property owning White men, but focus on the words property owning.

The right to vote and manipulate the mechanisms around voting were the key to certain groups maintaining power and it took place at state and local levels. There were constant legislative and court battles centered around different measures that some say are designed to make it more difficult for some groups to vote, register to vote and maintain their names on voter rolls in between elections. Another method used to allow certain groups that were shrinking in population representation in certain geographical areas to maintain political control was gerrymandering. Gerrymandering allows state election officials from the party in control to draw congressional voting districts so that they can negate the effect of racial changes in a county for example. Gerrymandering was used to prevent minorities from gaining additional seats at the table in county, state and national legislative bodies by drawing district boundaries that would group more minorities together, for example, so they would not gain an additional elected representative. Those redrawn district lines would often make no sense geographically in order for them to produce the election results desired by the political group in charge. Court challenges were making it difficult to continue with blatant tactics to ensure the continued election of White politicians when the demographics of the United States were shifting towards a majority minority population mix. The business of winning elections to keep the right people in charge was becoming too difficult and the election of Donald Trump was an unexpected gift for those invested in government for profit otherwise known as the modern day property owners. Those supporting Donald Trump were needed to get him elected and they played their part and anything afterward was to keep them placated.

The property owners that hold power today are the billionaires, massive corporations and lobbyists that fund the campaigns of politicians in exchange for them enacting policies favorable to their financial interests. Before everyone was allowed to vote, only White male property owners could vote because they held most of the wealth and power in the United States. Some may say that there was no resemblance to what happened in recent elections to those days when only White male property owners could vote, but that was where the error was made. When only a select category of individual could vote that meant everyone else had to live with policies and laws enacted by elected officials that were made without consideration of how they would react because they didn't matter for the next election cycle. While it was true that everyone could vote that was eligible in modern elections, regardless of property ownership, that only mattered for the election in the case of those politicians beholden to their donors more than the voting public. The voting public was manipulated and driven to vote on emotional issues such as abortion, immigration and cultural changes that usually divide voters into their political party preferences.

The Presidential election of 2016 had the additional elements of racial resentment and nationalism thrown into the mix. Donald Trump was elected Present because he said he would make America great again and he did for the new class of White male property owners defined as large corporations and investors.

As in all investigations the best way to determine what happened was to follow the money and there was the secret to the age of White reparations we were in the midst of experiencing. On December 22, 2017 Republican President Donald J. Trump signed a new tax bill into law that was a rewrite of the tax code of the United States. The new Republican written tax plan lowered both individual and corporate tax rates. The primary point pushed out to American citizens was that they would pay less in taxes. Critics of the plan stated that it would explode the debt of the United States since less tax revenue would come in to pay government obligations.

Class warfare debates erupted over the new tax code with opponents stating that most of the benefits went to the wealthy through a doubling of the estate tax exemption from $5 million to $10 million and lower corporate tax rate among other changes that favored high income earners with equity investments. Proponents of the new plan argued that companies would use the additional profits to invest in new jobs and higher wages for employees. The non-partisan Congressional Budget Office issued its analysis of the new tax plan on November 17, 2017 and the following is an excerpt:

The legislation would permanently modify business taxation as well. Among other provisions, beginning in 2019, it would replace the structure of corporate income tax rates, which has a top rate of 35 percent under current law, with a single 20 percent rate. The legislation also would substantially alter the current system under which the worldwide income of U.S. corporations is subject to taxation.

The staff of the Joint Committee on Taxation (JCT) estimates that enacting the legislation would reduce revenues by about $1,633 billion and decrease outlays by $219 billion over the 2018-2027 period, leading to an increase in the deficit of $1,414 billion over the next 10 years.
https://www.cbo.gov/system/files/115th-congress-2017-2018/costestimate/reconciliationrecommendationssfc.pdf

The magic number from the CBO report was the almost $1.5 trillion dollar increase in the federal deficit. Where would that $1.5 trillion go? Backers of the bill stated that the extra revenue would be invested in new business activity and growth from that would compensate for the reduced tax revenue along with increased wages from companies investing in their employees. Reality can be like a cold bucket of water thrown in someone's face to wake them up. Some companies paid one time bonuses to employees that were highly publicized, but even with near full employment, wage growth did not materialize. It appeared that the additional revenue flowing into corporate coffers was not being tricked down to the masses, but instead companies bought back their own stock and paid dividends to shareholders.

Several months into 2018, Republican United States Senator Marco Rubio from Florida confirmed how the new tax plan was working with comments he made in an interview confirming that corporations used their windfall from the tax cuts to buy back shares and pay a few bonuses, but did not invest in workers. The time window was closing for donor owned politicians to be able to maintain political power by legitimate means in order to provide the big payoffs demanded by their financial supporters. The unexpected opportunity Republicans had with Trump as President combined with control of both houses of Congress would not go to waste.

Reparation payments to the real property owners were in progress. Some might object and say they were property owners also, but that was not based upon the fact that individuals might own a home or vehicle. The keys to collecting those reparations were based upon being properly positioned financially to maximize ones take of the $1.5 trillion dollar windfall. The other rebuttal would be that there was nothing to restrict the revenue flow to White men only, but that was only technically accurate. When net wealth in the United States was examined based upon race then it was clear who was positioned to gain more from the new tax plan that at its core was a massive transfer of wealth from the bottom to the top. The 2016 Recent Trends in Wealth-Holding by Race and Ethnicity: Evidence from the Survey of Consumer Finances prepared by the Board of Governors of the Federal Reserve shows the wealth breakdown in the United States by race:

**Recent trends in wealth-holding**
We first analyze trends in total net worth among families classified, according to their self-identification during the interview, as white non-Hispanic, black or African American non-Hispanic, Hispanic or Latino, and other or multiple race (we will henceforth refer to these groups as white, black, Hispanic, and other, respectively).[1] Net worth is defined as the difference between families' gross assets and their liabilities.[2] We will describe patterns at the median (the typical household within each group) and at the mean (the average within each group).

In 2016, white families had the highest level of both median and mean family wealth: $171,000 and $933,700, respectively (figure 1). Black and Hispanic families have considerably less wealth than white families. Black families' median and mean net worth is less than 15 percent that of white families, at $17,600 and $138,200, respectively. Hispanic families' median and mean net worth was

$20,700 and $191,200, respectively. Other families--a diverse group that includes those identifying as Asian, American Indian, Alaska Native, Native Hawaiian, Pacific Islander, other race, and all respondents reporting more than one racial identification--have lower net worth than white families but higher net worth than black and Hispanic families. The same patterns of inequality in the distribution of wealth across all families are also evident within race/ethnicity groups: For each of the four race/ethnicity groups, the mean is substantially higher than the median, reflecting the concentration of wealth at the top of the wealth distribution.

**Figure 1: Net worth by race/ethnicity, 2016 survey**

Thousands of 2016 dollars

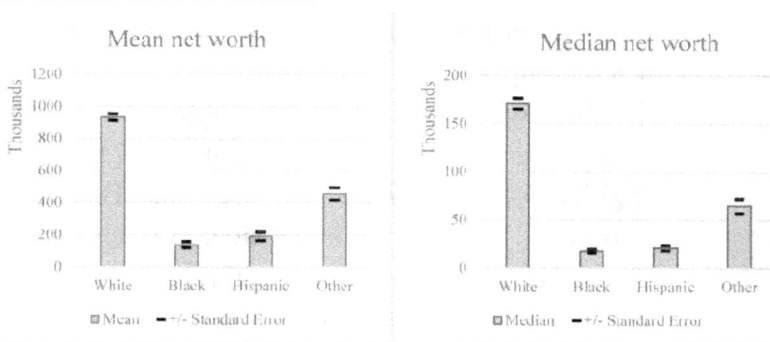

Source: Federal Reserve Board, Survey of Consumer Finances.

Between 2013 and 2016, median net worth rose for all groups (figure 2). Growth rates for the 2013-16 period were proportionally larger for Hispanic, other, and black families, rising between 30 and 50 percent, compared with white families, whose net worth rose 17 percent. Even with the large percentage gains for black and Hispanic families, the white-black gap in median net worth increased from $132,800 in 2013 to $153,500 in 2016, and the white-Hispanic gap increased from $132,200 in 2013 to $150,300 in 2016.

https://www.federalreserve.gov/econres/notes/feds-notes/recent-trends-in-wealth-holding-by-race-and-ethnicity-evidence-from-the-survey-of-consumer-finances-20170927.htm

The Following is an excerpt from the Congressional Budget Office – Trends in Family Wealth Survey, 1989 to 2013:

From 1989 to 2013, family wealth grew at significantly different rates for different segments of the U.S. population, and the distribution among the nation's families was more unequal in 2013 than it had been in 1989.

## Holdings of Family Wealth

Trillions of 2013 Dollars

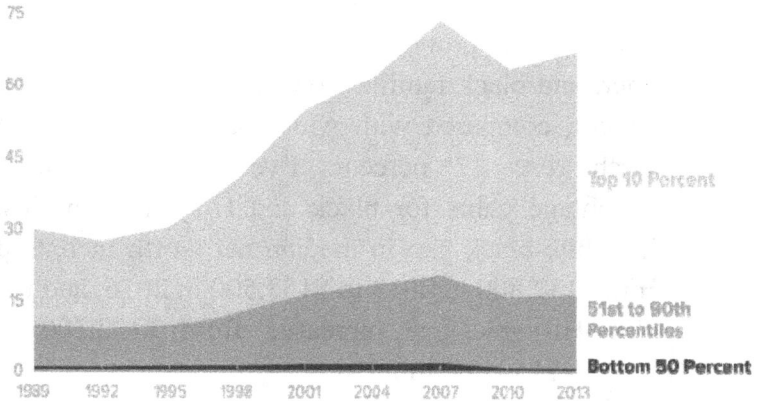

### How Is the Nation's Wealth Distributed?

In 2013, families in the top 10 percent of the wealth distribution held 76 percent of all family wealth, families in the 51st to the 90th percentiles held 23 percent, and those in the bottom half of the distribution held 1 percent. Average wealth was about $4 million for families in the top 10 percent of the wealth distribution, $316,000 for families in the 51st to 90th percentiles, and $36,000 for families in the 26th to 50th percentiles. On average, families at or below the 25th percentile were $13,000 in debt.

https://www.cbo.gov/publication/51846

114

After reviewing the wealth distribution by race it was sobering when comparing the net worth of White, Black and Hispanic families. The wealth disparity between White, Black and Hispanic households was staggering and as evidenced by the data in those government studies it became clear how simple it was to set up a functional reparations payment system for White Americans based upon their wealth status. The tax plan signed into law in 2017 rewarded wealth holders. Those with more investments, assets to pass on to heirs and large corporations will reap windfalls while saddling those unfortunate enough to be unable to take advantage of asset shielding provisions of the tax plan with the future debt. While not explicitly a plan to only pay Whites, it became heavily skewed in that direct due to the racial breakdown of wealth distribution in the United States. Those in the top 10 percent of family wealth holders in American own 76 percent of all family wealth in the nation and will score a literal bonanza from lower tax rates and other factors reflected in the tax code that rewarded high net worth individuals.

The bottom to top wealth transfer reflected in the tax regulations were color blind as written, but favored one race over others in execution based upon the wealth distribution in the United States with White families being multiple times wealthier than Blacks and Hispanics. Many White people will not be rewarded with financial reparations from the new tax plan unless they were wealthy enough participate in the windfall.

Understanding that tens of thousands to millions more dollars will be pumped into the bank accounts of wealthy individuals explained the blind loyalty and silence of those some thought would speak out against certain cruel social policies being enacted. Buying silence is an old practice and was working as planned on those selling their morality for money, but what about the people left out of sharing in the slush fund.

Why were Whites who were slavishly devoted to President Donald Trump ignoring his plethora of provable falsehoods, divisiveness and vulgarities? Why did Trump's many moral failings he was accused of, hush money payoffs to silence women about extramarital sexual affairs and multiple legal entanglements not ruffle feathers among his supporters? Why did Trump's supporters not make an outcry over the President of the United States breaking bonds and quarrelling with long standing allies while cozying up to brutal despots like Korea's Kim Jong Un, Russia's Vladimir Putin and Philippine's President Rodrigo Duterte who all have the blood of their citizens on their hands? Why did many Trump supporters stand by as a policy cloaked as immigration policy purposely separated adults crossing into the United States over the southwestern border with Mexico from their children as a matter of policy? Why would Trump supporters tolerate images of immigrant children warehoused in wire mesh pens at the hands of government agents at the behest of the highest officials in the United States government as they were broadcast worldwide? Why would Trump supporters tolerate the Attorney General of the United States, Jeff Sessions, quoting a taken out of context Bible verse, Romans 13, to justify taking immigrant children from their families because it was the law when in fact it was a policy that Sessions had announce earlier. The same bible verse Sessions quoted was used to justify slavery because it was the law along with other atrocities throughout history. The answer was wealthy Trump supporters, who often were going incognito, cared more about their pockets being lined from a huge bottom to top wealth transfer via the new tax plan. Trump supporters not positioned to benefit from a tax windfall bonanza were still hanging on for deliverance on job promises, but enjoyed psychological benefits of having a vocal advocate in the White House or relishing in the blatant display of White supremacy in action.

Eventually, the long suffering Trump supporters waiting on their employment prospects to improve in the heartland will lose patience and turn on their purported savior and his political supporters. Those enjoying having the President of the United States providing them with rallying cries might continue to support Trump if they were satisfied with their economic situations, but not if their cupboards were bare.

The bedrock Trump supporters that would never leave him were the hardcore racists and White Supremacists fighting the culture and racial wars. Trump was inflicting racial and cultural pain on a national level like they had not witnessed in decades. Trump was defending Confederate Monuments, slapping down Black athletes for kneeling during the national anthem and dishing out cruel treatment for immigrants daring to cross the southwestern United States border. Instead of bowing to pressure due to liberal backlash to curb some of his harsher tendencies, Trump would redouble his resolve and go even further with draconian policies and attacks.

Trump's base will fracture to the point that it would be unsustainable for his election to a second term, but that will not matter because his intent was never to be a President that served the interests of the average citizen of any race, religion or political party.

10

When Donald J. Trump unexpectedly became President of the United States he did so with the same attitude he did as in his business career. Trump approached the Presidency not as a public servant eager to preserve, protect and defend the Constitution of the United States, but as a corporate raider seeking to maximize returns to his political investors. When a corporate raider takes over a targeted company he shuts off revenue outflows, determines asset value, sells off or shuts down money losing divisions and finally liquidates everything else for maximum return. Employees and their jobs do not figure in the profit equation for a corporate raider and are expendable.

Trump began his Presidency with the perception of the United States as the greatest corporate takeover target in the history of the world and he wanted to leave his mark on history. Imagine the purposeful bankrupting of a county for selective profit of the American oligarchy comprised of special interest donors, wealthy individuals and corporate interests. Trump had the assistance of both houses of Congress under control of the Republican Party and lawmakers chose not to oppose actions undertaken by the President out of fears of political retribution at the ballot box during the next election cycle. Due to Republicans in

Congress surrendering their role of oversight of the Executive Branch of the United States in order to attain their policy agenda, Donald Trump assumed a posture as the President with the most unchecked power in modern history. Congress was empowered by the Constitution to be equal to the Executive Branch of Government in order to prevent a President from wielding unrestrained power like a king or dictator, but that only worked if Congress placed the interests of the country over their political party or thirst for political power.

The trade wars, conflicts with NATO allies and proposed curtailing of United States foreign aid to developing nations were all a part of the corporate raiding tactics of reducing spending that was viewed by Trump as wasteful. The Republican tax plan that starves the federal government coffers and directs copious amounts of money from lower income earners into the pockets of the wealthy was to set the stage for economic collapse and asset seizure. After the tax plan explodes the federal deficit, calls will go out to use the real nuclear option of raiding the Social Security and Medicare trust funds to save the economy from total collapse. Those at the top will have the resources to pick up the pieces of the American economy at bargain basement prices and wait for the slow crawl back to economic viability when they will profit greatly, again. Those left out in the cold, including those

Trump supporters who woke up too late to save themselves will wallow in sorrow with ruined lives along with many of the people they abhorred because of their race, religion or country of origin.

The age of White reparations was for the rich, the real property owners that mattered to Trump and his multibillion dollar supporters. To those sitting on top of the mountain the rest of us looked like ants at the bottom. Our healthcare, our standard of living and our thoughts of a moral America were impediments to greater goals driven by greed. Our crumbling roads, railways and airports were viewed as wasteful spending. Whether we fumed over small migrant children crying for their parents, were incensed over racist comments coming from the oval office or marveled at the destruction of the image of the United States as a principled leader in the world, it simply did not matter due to the ultimate goal being the plundering of the treasure of the nation.

The United States as we knew it was in grave danger because a man was placed into the ultimate position of political power in the United States out of a spirit of vengeance and the most vengeful man possible was elected. When a man became President who held nothing sacred including truth, loyalty, fidelity or patriotism, there was no good outcome for those embracing those qualities. The structures that formed the very pillars of the nation were under attack from the most powerful man in the world as he sought to destroy the credibility of all opposing him including the free press, judicial system and even departments of government in his direct reporting structure. Trump's credibility was known to be steeped in provable lies, so Trump, like many dictators was seeking to substitute blind loyalty for truth.

We pushed the United States down the slippery slope by enough of us following a man that was willing to allow our greatest enemy, Russia, to attack the core of our democracy though interfering with the 2016 Presidential election and let them get away with it because it helped him win. The intelligence agencies of the United States were attacked as the sitting President of the United States attempted to discredit them over their reports of Russia interfering in our elections in order to help elect Donald Trump. As a special prosecutor investigated whether the Trump campaign coordinated with Russians in intervening in the 2016 Presidential election on Trump's behalf, the President became more erratic as indictments, charges and guilty pleas drew ever closer to the oval office.

Facts lost their power under Trump and were replaced by fantasy, deflection and redirection that Trump supporters chose to accept in order to stay in his good graces while keeping their faint hopes alive.

There was a price to be paid by those that blindly excused the unpredictable tweets, policy shifts and international trade disputes because he would take them one step too far and then it happened. Attorney General Jeffrey Beauregard Sessions announced that there would be a zero tolerance policy for illegal immigrants entering the United States and they would have their children separated from them. Stories, images and sounds of children separated from their parents began to filter out from various detainment facilities filled with children in large chain link wire metal pens. Audio of crying children calling for their parents and callous responses from Trump administration officials in charge of the operation along with seeming indifference from the President sparked a fierce backlash from the public. Republican politicians, religious leaders and even some Trump supporters were repulsed by policies and images coming out of the United States that were reminders of concentration and internment camps from World War II, but it was too late. Republicans in Congress and religious leaders who supported or stayed quiet through the son of a bitch vulgarity hurled at Black athletes, the people from shithole countries comment about protected status immigrants and years long birther smear of Barack Obama were tied to Trump for better or worse.

Senator Ted Cruz, who swallowed his pride after candidate Trump attacked his family during the election to support him, came up with a legislation proposal to stop migrant child separations, although Trump could end the policy he implemented with a phone call, but it was too late for Cruz and the rest. Cruz and other Republican politicians were like passengers on a flight piloted by Donald Trump and it was much easier to get on board than to get off.

In order to get a Supreme Court Justice and a trickle up tax plan, Republicans went to a crossroads, like legendary blues musician Robert Johnson who made a deal with the devil, and made a deal with Donald J. Trump to get what they had always wanted. After the glow of the Supreme Court Justice and tax plan dimmed, Trump went off course and took Republicans on a flight to places they didn't want to visit when he attacked defenseless children fleeing crime, poverty and abuse along with their parents. Republicans wanted to just reject one particular outrage that repulsed Americans in general, but how could they reject part of Trump without rejecting all of Trump. Evangelical leaders wanted out of being seen as being supportive of forced child separations as a government policy, but they had excused every other Trump transgression that violated their teachings. Trump would pull those tied to him into the sewer while leaving a permanent stain on the soul of the United States unless they took drastic action and jumped out of the nearest exit and allowed him to crash on his own while they saved the nation.

To be clear, a majority of Republicans still supported Trump's child separation policy, but it was much lower that his overall support among his political party members. Trump may have found the antidote that broke the cult like hold he wielded over his supporters and it was state sponsored child abuse, but would that be enough to overcome the allure of White reparations. We could only hope.

God bless the United States of America.

Side Piece
Side Piece 2 – Amber Alarm
Hero In The Hood
The Pastor's Lover 2
She Twerks Hard For The Money
The Pastor's Lover 3
Forget Big Brother We Tell DAD
Everything
The Pastor's Wife 3
Hoe Hoe Hoe Merry Christmas
Ghetto Tony and White Trash Tina
Fifty Shades of Plaid
Grandma Does It Better
Keisha's Mama Is So Fine
Less Pretty
Pretty For A Dark Skinned Woman
Massive Monroe
The Pastor's Lover 4 – The Pastor's Wife 4
The Obituary of Gut Bucket Johnson
Forget Big Brother – We Tell DAD
Everything
Unreal Housewives of South Dallas
Liquid Memories: You Can Live Forever
Gold Digger's Game
Ebola – Partying With Grace
THOT On The Beach
What Would Dr King Think About Today's
Black America

Your Best Friend's Mother 2 – Lust In
London
Secrets of a Baby Mama
Secrets of a Baby Mama 2
Trump – Nixon on Steroids – Stay Woke
Chocoholic

www.ingramcontent.com/pod-product-compliance
Lightning Source LLC
Chambersburg PA
CBHW071338290326
41933CB00039B/1479

*9 780982 460696*